BOYS ON THE EDGE

BOYS ON THE EDGE

A Coming of Age Memoir on the Outer Banks

SAM BASS JR.

For more information, contact: https://storiesfromthebanks.com/contact

Edited by Jane Langley Brothers and JB Parker
Cover Art by Glen Lamp
Cover Design by Nejc Planinšek

First edition March 2024

ISBN 979-8-9902407-0-4 (hardcover)
ISBN 979-8-9902407-1-1 (paperback)
ISBN 979-8-9902407-2-8 (ebook)

The Library of Congress Cataloging-in-Publication data is on file with the publisher.

boysontheedge.com

To my brother Clyde.
You danced magnificently along the Edge.

TABLE OF CONTENTS

Introduction

In the summer of 1969, our country was on edge, with widespread violence over civil rights, racial desegregation, and war in Vietnam. If a day went by without news from one of these, the Cold War filled in with the ever present threat of atomic annihilation. Russia and the United States built huge nuclear arsenals and raced for technological superiority in space for mutual assured destruction — MAD. Regardless of who fired first, both countries would cease to exist.

During this chaotic time, my brother, cousin, and I planned to spend an un-parented three months on a remote, sparsely inhabited island on the southernmost part of the North Carolina Outer Banks, called Cape Lookout. All worries would be behind us, or so we thought.

Old timers refer to the Outer Banks of North Carolina as the 'Edge.' Jutting far into the stormy North Atlantic, the islands create a treacherous region of shoals and unforgiving ocean currents that can be perilous for ships. Since the sixteenth century, some 5,000 vessels have gone down in those waters, earning it the name "Graveyard of the Atlantic."

During our summer on the island, we blurred the lines between fun and foolhardiness, life and death, and love and loss. We struggled with anger, shame, guilt, suicide, and the riptides of emotions between fathers and sons. Through our triumphs over natural adversities and those we caused ourselves, we grew closer and learned to depend on each other. Our cuts and bruises became external badges of the healing of emotional wounds that we'd entrusted to each other and to God.

When considering the period for this memoir, one stood out among all the rest. The year of my driver's license. The freedom to go anywhere, any time, and to listen to music at any volume I wanted was exactly what I needed to escape the worst of 1969 for the best of 1969.

A car was the ultimate sound machine, and the year produced some of the very best American music ever. Billboard's top hits ranged from folk to Motown, to California surf, war protest, bubblegum, rock, hard rock, and hallucinogenic. Cass Elliott, Stevie Wonder, the Beach Boys, and The Rolling Stones forged ahead. Bob Dylan, Edwin Starr, Deep Purple, Procol Harum, Jimmy Hendrix, and others, opened new frontiers. The incredible decade of music development culminated in the fall of '69 with a rock concert on a farm in upstate New York, called Woodstock.

On July 20, 1969, amidst all the chaos, America accomplished the incredible feat of putting men on the moon and bringing them home again. "For one price-less moment in the whole history of man, all the people on this Earth are truly one," President Nixon said to Neil Armstrong and Buzz Aldrin as they walked on the moon.

Scattered through this story are bits of family history and perspective of the events and communications that led to the establishment of the Cape Lookout National Seashore. Many are marked with superscript numbers that reference notes at the end of the book offering more complete descriptions.

Reliving experiences from the summer of '69, percolated through sixty years of life's grounds, revealed rich insights into the relationships that have shaped me. A strange thing happened while surfing through these long-buried memories for the sights, sounds, smells, feelings, and emotions needed to bring this story to life. Once dim shadows of characters from my past, came back to life as complex, beautifully flawed, loving people who shaped my life.

This story is true to the best of my recollections of the events and people. Where I felt more information was needed, I sought the memories of others, as well as letters and documents. Names and events are changed in two significant places in the story. The first instance is to protect the privacy of an individual and the second is to create a literary device that gathers critical elements into a more cohesive, impactful conclusion. These two instances are explained in disclosures at the end of the book in the Notes section. You have the choice of spoiling the story by reading those disclosures now or after you enjoy the story as written by your faithful author.

And now, please allow me to transport you back to a beautiful and dangerous place during the summer of 1969, where four boys pressed very hard against and into the edges of manhood.

one

Summer's Here!

The bell finally rang. A rough school year ended, and summer vacation was finally here. Eager to get to my Mustang, I pushed and shoved my way through the sweltering classroom into the hall. Hopes for a quick exit vanished when I saw the mass of students between me and the exits. My shirt stuck to me as kids bumped and pushed from all sides. The noise, chaos, and sour air was a fitting end to the year. I couldn't wait to escape and get on the road.

Reaching the doors and twisting free of the crowd, I took a deep breath and bolted for the sophomore parking lot, shouting goodbyes along the way. When I saw my brother Clyde standing by the car, I knew we could beat the traffic out of the parking lot.

"Let's go to the Cape." Clyde shouted.

Tossing my book bag into the back, I jumped into the bright red driver's seat and jammed the key into the ignition. Clyde slid through the window, and cranked up the radio with Steppenwolf screaming, "Born to be Wild."

A shot ran through me as the engine rumbled to life. I slammed the shifter into first and popped the clutch for a satisfying squawk of the tires. Clyde leaned over and spoke loudly enough to be heard over the radio, "Take it easy brother, there're a lot of people around here."

Nodding, I slowed, amused at the irony of my crazy little brother urging *me* to be careful. When we came to the main road, Clyde, truer to form, shouted *"Throw it in her."*

His words were gasoline on weeks of smoldering anticipation. An entire summer of adventure awaited us on a remote island on the eastern edge of North Carolina, called Cape Lookout. I kicked the Mustang hard, and she responded with instant fury. Tires squealed and smoke billowed to leave a huge dusty blue cloud that engulfed the long line of cars behind us.

The spectacle caught the full attention of the girls in a powder-blue VW slug-bus ahead of us. In it were Kay O'Riley and five of the best-looking varsity cheerleaders. They waved, shouted, and blew full-lipped kisses as we sped by.

Wow, did they even halfway mean those kisses?

"That's one silly-ass grin on your face, Sam."

"Yeah, it's so cool to be noticed by those girls. They act so stuck-up in the halls. It's like it hurts them to say hello. Maybe they'll be nicer next year."

"Dream on brother," he said as he cranked up the volume to "Venus," by the Shocking Blue.

Windows down, radio blasting, all that stood between us, and the Cape, was picking up our cousin John at his family's farm on the other side of town. He had just returned from Virginia Episcopal School. His father had pulled him out of Sanford Central High when the riots and chaos of integration broke out.

The farm was our second home. There, we learned to milk cows, ride horses, bail hay, slaughter pigs, mend fences, and drive very, very fast on acres and acres of rolling grassy pastures. Our driving skills were honed by the long hours of high-speed 360s, sideways spins, jumps, and other fun not allowed on small-town streets.

Approaching the farm entrance, I slowed to make the turn through the gate. The familiar rumble of the tires crossing the steel cattle guards never got old. We were on the farm.

The winding tree-lined drive climbed a gentle hill for a quarter mile or so. The aromas of fresh cut grass, flowering magnolias, and grazing cattle floated through the car as we sped by.

How fun it would be to peel off into that lush green pasture—wide open—like so many times before. But the car was clean, and she was mine now. Mom had given me the keys to her 1964½ Mustang on my birthday, two months earlier. I'd spent almost as much time polishing as driving her.

Near the top of the ridge, the beautiful brick Georgian home came into view. Beyond the tennis court was a gate to a drive that encircled the house. As we passed across the cattle guards onto the drive, we saw Aunt Sarah standing over a stack of supplies behind the house. "Oh man, we can't fit all that stuff in the car," Clyde said.

Aunt Sarah had this amazing presence. She seemed to float above the chaos of farm life stirred by three rambunctious sons, and a beautiful, horse-loving, tomboy of a daughter, named Suzanne, who galloped through life with little regard for girly stuff. But our aunt's patience had a limit, and we were experts in discovering it. Her discipline was swift and fierce.

She was beautiful. She won both the Miss North Carolina and Miss South Carolina titles in her teens. After marriage, she and Uncle Charlie moved to New York, where she pursued a career in film, radio, and modeling. When WWII broke out in 1941, Uncle Charlie joined the Navy and she moved back to her hometown in Chester, South Carolina. After the war, they began building a family and a life on the Reeves Ridge Farm.

Clyde jumped out of the car and ran around the back before we'd stopped. "Hi Aunt Sarah," he said, hugging her. "I've missed seeing you with John away at school."

Smiling, she said, "That's sweet Clyde, I've missed you boys too. Of course, you may get more of us than you want when we visit the Cape in July."

Just then, John burst through the screened kitchen door with large bundles of bed sheets, wrapped in brown paper.

3

"Hello Clyde, Sam, good to see you guys," John said in his playful sarcasm. It was a tone easily taken as arrogance by anyone unfamiliar with his speaking style.

"Hey John," I responded. "You've grown some. Looks like VES feeds you well. You ready to hit the Cape?"

Hell yeah . . . "Sorry Mother, that slipped," he said, chuckling through his nose.

"Maybe boarding school has done you more harm than good, mister," Aunt Sarah scolded.

Turning to Clyde, I whispered, "Let's get this stuff loaded and hit the road."

Moments later, a hand was on my shoulder. It was Aunt Sarah. "Sam, you are the oldest. Set a good example for the boys. Drive carefully, make good decisions, and don't egg them on."

How many times would I fall short on that?

"Yes ma'am," I said, sounding a little apologetic.

John crammed the last bag into the trunk and forced it shut. We gave Aunt Sarah a hug, encouraged her not to worry, and slid into the three remaining pockets of space in the car. John took the front seat, knowing there was no way he'd fit into the back, even if it was empty.

"Be careful boys," Aunt Sarah implored as I started the car.

John quipped, "Mom, when have we ever *not* been careful?"

Her eyes flashed and she leaned into my window. In her firmest tone she said, "John Reeves, it's not too late for me to change your plans."

He smiled and offered a more respectful, "Luuve you mom. We'll be careful."

As we pulled away, I was sure there was a grin on her face. A mother's love for her boys has to be the most enduring quality on earth. No matter how often we test them, their love never wavers. We didn't deserve them.

When we were out of sight of the house, I kicked it, and Clyde cranked up the radio blasting the drums and guitars of "Hawaii Five-O" by the Vogues, over the wind and road noise.

4

Coming to the highway leading out of town, I yelled, "We'll be on the Cape in five hours."

"Seven hours if we don't leave the dock at least thirty minutes before dark. It's too easy to run aground in the shallows on a low-tide night," John said.

Just then, The Doors started "Hello I Love You." I shouted, "Then what are we waiting for?" Slamming it into second, I squealed the tires. "To the Cape!"

The miles rolled by as we sang top-40 songs and delighted in the parade of Coppertone and Sea & Ski billboards of bronzed, bikinied beach babes.

Passing a road sign for Havelock, I said, "Hey we'll be at the Red & White soon. Let's make out a grocery list so we can breeze through."

"Good, my legs are going to sleep in this little car," John said.

"Try it back here, you ass. I haven't felt mine since Mount Olive." Clyde fired back.

Feeling disrespected, I said, "I'm quite comfortable, *thank you very much*. If you buttheads want to try your thumbs for something better, I'll gladly pull over."

John grunted and reached into the glovebox. Finding a pencil, he tore off part of a roadmap and we began making a list of essentials. It included cases of soda, SpaghettiOs, Chef Boyardee pizza kits, Slim Jims, peanut butter, and cookies.

As we pulled into the Red & White parking lot, John tore the list into three parts and said, "Let's divide and conquer."

When we regrouped at the front of the store, we realized there was not enough room in the car to carry our bounty, so we set aside the least essential items. Clyde and I returned them while John checked out, charging the total to the house account.

With some repacking and lots of jamming, we eventually got the groceries loaded and pulled back onto the road. After a couple of blocks, we turned onto NC 101, which paralleled the Marine airfield. Signs of civilization were soon replaced by forests and salt marshes. We made good time, until the pavement narrowed and began to wind unpredictably.

two

Down East

Slowing to meet the demands of the road, we relaxed in the warm, evening air. It was filled with earthy scents of fresh-plowed fields, fertilizer, and the unmistakable salty air of the Atlantic, just a few miles ahead. We were in the low country of eastern North Carolina, a uniquely beautiful part of our state, as distinct as the people who live there. Soaking in the sights and smells, I wondered what it would be like to grow up here, in this simpler yester-world known as Down East.

Cars, trucks, and farm tractors pulled in front of us, as suited them. It would have angered us at home, but not here. We hardly noticed slipping into our own down-east summer groove.

The sunlight softened and tunes mellowed with "Get Together" by the Youngbloods. The Mustang effortlessly carved her way through the turns, following the rhythms and inflections of the music. The song expressed hope for a country ripped apart by race, war, and politics.

My mind at that moment was on the billboard visions of bikinied blondes and the hoped-for possibility of meeting one this summer. Around the next curve, the thought vanished when the Harkers Island bridge appeared in the distance, across the expanse of salt marshes.

As unique as Down East was, our island destination was in a class of its own. Settled by Scottish immigrants in the early 1700s, the people had changed little since then. Many islanders were direct descendants of the original settlers. Their brogue and attitudes echoed those of their middle-English forebears.

Most were fishermen and boatbuilders. They reluctantly tolerated a few dozen weekend fishermen who stayed in the two motel-marinas known as Harkers Motel and Hills Marina. The islanders referred to anyone who wasn't born there as 'Dit Dots,' or 'Off.' If you weren't one of them, you were simply – 'Off.'

At the bridge, I slowed to an idle. A couple of small boys skim-boarded along the shoreline. Dank scents of marsh grass and oysters filled the car as conversations and laughter surrounded us.

Most folks stood near the rails as they fished and chatted. Some, aware of our approach, moved aside, while others turned away ignoring our interruption. A little further down, we rolled to a full stop for a group of old timers who occupied the better part of both lanes with their coolers, bait buckets, and fishing gear. Harkers Island, after all, was *their* island, and this was *their* bridge. Our parents taught us to respect them as our hosts. But we didn't feel welcome, so far anyway.

Sitting there, with the engine idling, a few made eye contact that we answered with nods. There was a wiry old salt in the middle of the group telling what must have been a fantastic tale, given the attention he'd earned by at least half the bridge's population. Minutes later, hoots of laughter signaled an end to the story. Enough of the group moved out of our lane, dragging their coolers and buckets with them to clear a path. We waved and said hellos as we weaved slowly through.

Once off the bridge, I sped up to about twenty-five to make our way along the Island Road. Charcoal smoke, juniper scents, and the laughter of children filled the cool evening air. Adults rocked and talked on their porches as the day's catches smoked on nearby grills. Kids pumped tire swings ever skyward, kicked balls, and called out "Red Rover, Red Rover."

Scattered among the houses and live oaks were huge metal buildings housing some of the most renowned sport-fishermen boat builders in the world. There was Rose Brothers, Lewis, Guthry, and Willis Boat Builders.

Nearing the end of the island, we spotted Hills Marina and pulled into the drive a little before seven. We had less than an hour's daylight and were anxious to load the boat and begin our seven-mile trip across the sound to the Cape. We were just as excited to see Mr. Credle.

He was like a favorite grandfather to us. He seemed to remember being a teenager better than most adults did. He rarely lectured us. When he did, we listened, especially when he spoke about the water.

After catching up on how our parents and how his daughter Mary Frances and son Travis were doing, he cut short our visit to say, "It's getting near dark. You'd better be on your way."

We agreed and after buying some milk and ice, headed for the door.

Mr. Credle reminded us, "When you get to the shallows, trust the sticks the local fisherman put up – not the buoys. The Coast Guard can't keep up with the shifts in the channel like the locals do."

"OK, thanks, Mr. Credle, We'll see you soon."

three

Whirlwind to the Cape

Driving around behind the motel to the long-term parking area, she came into view, floating patiently in her slip. The Whirlwind was a graceful 24-foot mahogany runabout with a mid-blue hull. She was designed for a life of leisure cruising, picnicking, and skiing, but had proven a stalwart workboat during the construction of the A-Frame house on the Cape and for its ongoing maintenance.

Six five-foot propane cylinders stamped TEELS GAS, stood on the dock, awaiting transport to the Cape. We laid them into the boat and stuffed our gear, groceries, and supplies between them to reduce their banging into each other on the open water. We used propane for cooking, heating, refrigeration, and lighting. When electricity was needed, we generated it with a large army surplus generator. The gasoline it and the vehicles required was hauled out in heavy 55-gallon drums.

Clyde flipped on the batteries and pumped the fuel line tight as I cleared the dock lines. Holding up crossed fingers, John turned the key. The large 150-horse Evinrude spun a few times, then rattled to life in a cloud of blue, honey-sweet smoke. Our boisterous "woo-hoos" disturbed a couple of nearby fishermen. They shook their heads and gave us the kind of look men give boys when they think they're having too much fun, without regard for the cost.

With a wave of apology, I called "All clear." John bumped the throttle ahead and we idled out of the slip and marina. Once in the open sound, we headed southward toward the Cape channel.

It was our final leg, the absolute best part of the trip. The sun was setting off our starboard side and would soon be below the horizon. The evening air was calm and cool. The tide was low but rising. At least if we ran aground, there would be more water coming to eventually lift us off the bottom.

Tides were an important consideration for boaters, especially near the Cape. There was a spot along the way called the shallows or the 'S-turns.' At low tide, navigable water was reduced to as little as a foot or two, in the middle of the channel. Our tides varied by as much as three feet every five hours, between high and low tides. Full and new moons added as much as six inches to the variance.

John rammed the throttle ahead and the bow of the Whirlwind rose high into the air. Moments later, our fully loaded boat reached a plane and was running wide open. We plowed through the rolling waves gracefully, except for the occasional clanging of propane tanks. A little more effort to secure them might have been advised, but we were anxious to get to the Cape, and they'd be fine.

John showed no concern at the shallows. He maintained full throttle as he confidently wove his way through the curves, stick by stick, red on the left and green on right. Some of them were well away from the official steel buoys. It was hard to think of an instance when John was short on confidence. Clyde or I could rattle off any number of occasions when his self-assuredness landed him, and us, in trouble.

There was a time, about a year ago, when we were driving on the farm in his brother David's old Rambler. John got this crazy idea to jump a creek running through the woods at the bottom of a steep hill. He was so sure he could do it, there was no chance of talking him out of it—even if we'd wanted to—and we didn't. It would be too much fun to watch.

"I'm gonna need to be going at least fifty miles an hour to clear that creek." John said, with a studious look.

"John, this old clunker takes five minutes to reach fifty." Clyde laughed.

"This steep hill will give us all the acceleration we'll need. "She'll do it," John said defiantly, suggesting his calculations were complete and he was ready to execute his plan.

"Hang on." John screamed and he floored the gas pedal.

Tires whined as they spun over the mossy roots and dirt. Seconds later, we were hurdling down the rutted hill. Clyde bounced between the seat and ceiling like a pinball.

Thuds, screams, and engine roar joined in a deafening din as we rocketed down the hill. Hitting the creek berm at the bottom felt like we would go right through the floorboard. Suddenly, we were drifting skyward. I was blinded by the sunlight sparkling through the trees. Then, for a couple of very cool seconds, we were weightless during our descent back to earth.

Our flight ended with a terrific crash and splash. Each of us slammed into the object that was directly in front of us. For John, it was the steering wheel. For me, the dash. And Clyde, the back of John's seat.

Shaking the stars out of our heads, we looked around and saw that we had not cleared the creek. We'd landed smack dab in the middle of it.

Clyde spoke up from the back seat—just as cool as you please— "Uh guys, take a look at this."

John and I turned around and kneeled on the seat to follow Clyde's pointing finger.

"Damn," John said.

Sticking up between Clyde's feet was a large tree trunk at the end of a long gash that started somewhere under John's seat. We exploded in laughter – until John grasped the full measure of the situation. "David's gonna kill me."

With that, Clyde and I busted out laughing again – in total agreement.

Safely through the shallows, the channel straightened and deepened. The damp salty air refreshed my face and lungs. A blazing orange sun nearing the horizon cast a soft golden hue on the sandy beaches and the white diamonds of the distant lighthouse. The sparkling ocean, back sounds, islets, golden dunes, and swaying sea oats were an enchanting paradise, apart from the chaotic world we'd left behind.

The portholes and roofing seams of the A-Frame were clearly visible, signaling that our journey was nearly over. Straining to see the dock, John said, "They're no boats tied up."

Our landing and unloading would be fast and trouble-free, or so we thought. When John pulled back on the throttle to approach, the island's dreaded blood-sucking no-see-ums attacked. The little demons swarmed without mercy, in overwhelming numbers to compensate for their small size. Moments later, a wave of mosquitoes attacked.

"These bastards are all over me," Clyde screamed.

"Yeah, they're in my eyes and ears too," I shouted. "John, what the hell are you doing?"

Seconds later, John popped up from the stern compartment, jammed a screwdriver into a can of motor oil, and poured the glistening goo generously into his hands. He quickly spread it over every bit of exposed skin, including his face. Then he smeared it into his hair, shirt, and pants.

He did it with such conviction that Clyde said, "What the hell, give me some of that." He filled his hand, then gave the can to me.

When we were completely covered with the slimy stuff, the attack ended. We burst into laughter, looking, and smelling like we'd fallen into a grease pit.

"Last summer, I noticed the mosquitoes and gnats didn't bother us in the Jeep shed. Thinking it might be the oil and gasoline fumes, seemed worth a try."

"Nice thinking," Clyde said. "Haven't had a bite, except my head. Guess I'll have to put this mess in my hair too."

With light fading, we secured the boat, hopped onto the dock, and began our quarter mile hike to the A-Frame. On the way we discussed what we needed to do to bring the house to life. John and Clyde were the mechanics and would start in the shed to get the equipment and vehicles running. John would open one of two banks of propane cylinders to supply the house appliances and lights with propane. He'd then start the generator and fill the freshwater tanks which hung in the peak of the A-Frame on the third floor.

Clyde would attempt to start one or both sometimes unreliable beach vehicles. One was a '42 Willys Jeep and the other was a '53 Willys with a large flat wooden bed for hauling gear and supplies. My job was to get the house opened up and light the appliance pilots.

It was almost pitch-black when we got to the house. The A-Frame rose high above us with its menacing, round, black windows. It had an other-worldly look in this light. The lighthouse's bright sweeping beam illuminated the house and dunes every twenty seconds or so. It reminded me of scenes from WWII movies in which the searchlights raked across the grounds of German prison-of-war camps.

We climbed over the high dune beside the house to reach the driveway. Clyde and John headed for the Jeep shed, and I walked toward the house, stepping gingerly over the twisted steel mats of the driveway. The giant 'A' structure towered above me as I climbed the dark back stairs. There was an eerie still on the back deck. How in the world had Cousin Suzanne stayed out here alone? I was scared stiff, and there were two other guys with me.

Pulling the key from my pocket, I grabbed the padlock on the door and pointed the bottom toward the lighthouse's next passing beam. Lots of effort was required to insert the key. The lock had stiffened from months' exposure to the salty ocean breezes. With a few twists and turns, it eventually snapped open.

I took a breath of courage, turned the doorknob, and gave the narrow door a bump with my shoulder to force it open. The cavernous house was void of light except for a dim grayness through the windows at the front of the A-Frame. The house was dead quiet. The air was hot and stale.

Sliding a hand along the cabinets I made my way down the hall. When the lighthouse beam flashed through the portholes, I mapped my path to the stove, across the kitchen floor. There was always a box of matches on the counter nearby. Finding it and striking a match, I held the flame to the propane wall lantern and opened the gas valve. With a pop, the room came to light. As light as something like a forty-watt bulb anyway.

After lighting a couple more, I turned my attention to the refrigerator and water heater pilot lights. Exactly how a propane refrigerator cooled and froze food was a mystery to me, but it worked very well, until the coils rusted out in the salty air. They rarely lasted more than two or three years on the Cape.

The next job was to open up the place to exhaust the tomb-like air – unstirred for months. The western side of the house faced the sound with floor-to-peak louvered windows that were operated by a long crank.

Most A-Frame houses have no openings on their side walls because of possible leaks. Regular windows can't hold out wind or rain when they are on a slant. But this house demanded light, air flow, and access to the beautiful vistas in all directions. A unique solution was needed.

Uncle Charlie and Dad had served in the South Pacific in the Navy during WWII. There, they learned firsthand the benefits of portholes. The circular bronze and glass windows kept sea and rain out when closed and yielded fresh, cool air below decks when opened. They decided that portholes would provide an ideal solution and found them in plentiful supply in a Wilmington salvage yard.

For all their benefits though, opening and closing them was a slow, messy, and laborious task. Four large bronze ringed bolts were loosened with a bar or large screwdriver. Once unbolted, the heavy bronze-encased glass was raised and hooked on a chain.

In my haste to let the fresh air in, I forgot about the sand and water that collects in the casing outside. Pulling the first one open dumped a load of wet sand over my oily hair, back and shoulders. The rest, I opened properly, with a bucket underneath.

When the flatbed roared to a start, I joined Clyde and John in the shed for our trip back to the boat. John came from behind the generator yelling, "The water tanks'll have to wait until tomorrow. I can't get this lousy generator to start."

"I'll take a look tomorrow," Clyde said. "Hop on, let's go."

The lights on the flatbed were hardly more than candles. But roads on the Cape were pretty easy to see at night. The bright white sand contrasted against the dark grassy boarders and dunes. The sweeping lighthouse beam helped too. The tide was a foot higher when we got back to the dock. Handing up the gear and tanks from the boat was much easier.

Mosquitoes no longer bothered us, making unloading the boat much easier than it might have been. On the way back to the house, I said, "Let's leave everything but the food and our bags on the truck tonight. We can unload the rest tomorrow. I'm starved."

Given the late hour, bugs, and our flammable insect repellant, we decided against grilling in favor of cooking inside. Clyde heated the beans, I cooked the steaks, and John made the salad. My transistor radio was tuned to WMBL, playing "What Does It Take to Win Your Love" by Jr. Walker & the All Stars. Stars filled the front windows and a gentle breeze swirled through the house making for a perfect end to an excellent trip to the Cape.

four

Beach Party

Bright beams of golden sunlight cast egg-shaped globes onto our bedroom wall. A wispy breeze rustled my sheets reminding me of dozens of bites from last night's mosquito attack. My sticky skin and waxy hair were added reminders of our fearsome island greeting.

Clyde and John were motionless. But it was time to start the day. Reaching for my transistor radio, a full turn of the volume knob delivered the hoped-for result. Strawberry Alarm Clock blasted into the room with "Incense and Peppermint." Reactions were fast and fun.

Clyde rolled over and hurled a pillow at the radio—or at me—but missed both.

"You sorry jerk. I was sound asleep. Turn that mess off."

John added a withering salvo of obscenities that could only have been learned at prep school. Reaching for my shorts, I lumbered down the outside stairs to the back deck to pee. The other two weren't far behind.

The house had six modern bathrooms, two of which had showers. Their number and quality made the house unique on Cape Lookout. But bathrooms required water and John had failed to start the generator and pump to fill the water tanks. Even when the toilets had water, we preferred to greet the morning outdoors.

In the kitchen, Clyde pulled a jar of sugar from the cabinet and began wrestling with it. Once he'd banged it open, he found the contents had turned to something like concrete and went about grinding and chipping. John pulled a large white paper bag marked **XXX** Puffed Wheat from the duffle on the kitchen floor and I grabbed a carton of milk from the fridge. By the time we sat down with bowls and spoons ready, Clyde had freed enough yellow chunks for a delicious breakfast. On the radio was a reporter at the NASA Space Center talking about final preparations for the Apollo 11 moon launch in July. I was a total nut for the space program and followed every Mercury, Gemini, and Apollo mission.

With his mouth stuffed with puffs, Clyde mumbled, "So what do we want to do today?"

"Walter won't be here until Wednesday, so we've got some time to play," John said.

Our summer's fun came with an obligation to keep the house running and supplied. Walter's visit was an important part of that. He was the Reeves' farm manager and was coming to teach us how to run the bulldozer to keep Uncle Charlie's landing field smooth and packed.

"Well, there's nothing going on around here," I said. "The Barden and Long cottages are shut up tight."

Both houses were in plain sight of the A-Frame. They sat inside a curve in the shoreline, referred to as the Bight by some and the Hook by others. The Cape looks like a fishhook on the chart.

While staring at the remaining wheat puffs in my bowl, it came to me. "Guys, I just remembered. Candice Perry invited us to drop by her cottage on Atlantic Beach any time this week, starting today. She's having a house party with a bunch of girls from school."

Clyde jumped up, "Then what are we waiting for?"

"Did she say who's coming?" John asked.

"Well, there's Carol, Ava, Rhonda, Connie, and Vicky. She has a cousin coming too."

"That's a great group," John said. "They're your crowd, aren't they?"

"Yeah. They're fun," I said.

Clyde cranked up the radio with Every Mother's Son singing, "Come on Down to My Boat Baby."

"The truck's still loaded from last night. Let's take the Jeep if it'll start," John said.

We jumped up from the table, tossed our bowls into the sink and headed for the shed. On the way out, we picked up a case of Check Colas, a handful of nabs, and I grabbed a bottle of dishwashing detergent.

Clyde pulled a wrench off the shed wall and flung open the Jeep's hood. In no time at all he'd connected the battery and checked the engine. "Hit the starter, John" Clyde shouted, from under the hood.

After a couple of turns, the flat-head four cylinder fired up, extremely loud within the confines of the shed. Mufflers were another piece of equipment that didn't last long in the Cape's salty air.

Grabbing the Taperflex and Alfredo Mendoza slalom skis off the truck bed and a ski rope from the shed wall, I tossed them into the back of the Jeep. Clyde slammed the hood shut, and yelled, "Dibs on skiing to Atlantic Beach."

"That's fourteen miles on the outside," John shouted. "No way."

"Yeah, barely enough time to get warmed up," Clyde yelled while jumping into the shotgun seat.

John rolled eyes and I smiled as he backed aggressively down the ramp and driveway. At the bottom, he floored the Jeep leaving a tall plume of sand, and we were off.

The Whirlwind was tied at the end of the dock, just as we'd left her the night before. Running toward the water and holding up the bottle of dishwashing detergent, I shouted, "I need to wash off last night's mosquito repellant before seeing the girls. Anyone care to join me?"

John and Clyde quickly followed me into the water.

Scrubbing his hair, Clyde said, "I want to ski off the dock."

John looked at him sideways and said, "Clyde, it's low tide. That drop's gotta be four feet. You crazy?"

"It's no skin off your butt, John. I want to try it."

"You got no sense, but you can't do it if you don't try it, right?"

Clean as we were going to get, we loaded our gear into the boat and motored around to Clyde. Holding the coiled ski rope, I said, "You're mighty far up there. You sure about this?"

"You two sound like a couple of ninnies. Let's go," Clyde snapped.

I tossed him the rope, and John chuckled and idled away from the dock. We left enough slack for the boat to gain momentum before yanking Clyde off the dock, without pulling his arms out of their sockets.

On Clyde's signal, with a huge cloud of smoke, the Evinrude roared ahead. The rope sprang like a rubber band and snatched Clyde off the dock headfirst, like Wylie Coyote tied to one of his ACME rockets. With no chance of getting the ski under him, he landed like a torpedo, bounced a couple of times, and then dived deep below the surface. When he came up, spitting seawater and gasping for air, John and I laughed too hard to ask if he was ok. We knew he was alright, when he joined us.

Show over, John circled around with the rope and on Clyde's signal, we were on our way. A few minutes later, we cleared the protection of the hook, and were rising and falling on the gentle swells of the ocean. Clyde couldn't get much air jumping the soft-topped swells, so he made some turns up and down their faces. We were sure he would wear himself out long before we reached Atlantic Beach.

The sky was clear blue, winds were light, and the temp was perfect. We were running wide open to a beach party full of pretty girls. The gold and green sea oats of Shackleford Banks rolled steadily past our starboard side. They were a beautiful, unspoiled edge of North Carolina's pristine coastline. Off the port side was the majestic, azure blue Atlantic Ocean. What a blessing it was to be out here, so far removed from our country's problems and the past school year.

A few months earlier, John and I had gone with Aunt Sarah to visit Washington D.C. We saw machine gun nests at every major intersection in the monuments district. She said they were there to discourage violence during the anti-war protests. How ironic, I thought, that weapons of war had to be used to keep the peace of anti-war marches.

The cool salty wind and warm sunlight brought me back to a more beautiful world. Clyde was having a blast jumping the growing swells. He showed no sign of tiring. John yelled over the engine and wind, "He's already gone longer than I thought he could, but he won't make it to Atlantic Beach."

Nodding, I said, "But he's sure raising the bar."

About a half an hour into our trip, we spotted the sea buoys marking the Beaufort Channel, followed by Fort Macon and the edge of Atlantic Beach. Clyde's jumping had given way to slow turns inside the boat's wake with his arms hooked in the ski handle to rest his exhausted hands. I motioned with a slice across my neck to see if he was ready to quit, but he scowled and made an abrupt turn across the wake to resume his cuts, like he had something to prove.

In the Beaufort Channel, about a quarter mile from shore, we could see the first row of cottages just beyond Tar Landing. The outgoing tide in the channel opposed by a stiffening southwesterly breeze, formed large, irregular waves. Both Clyde and the outboard strained as they plowed through the chop. Clyde motioned to speed up for some jumps, but John shook his head and yelled to me that he was going as fast as he could.

Once across the inlet and beyond the fort's rock jetty, we headed toward the beach to run parallel along the shore, just outside the breakers. Our course took us close to a few swimmers who had ventured out into the deep water. Pointing out the Perry cottage to John, I said, "It's the brick one, this side of the white cottages."

In front were a volleyball net, a couple of guys tossing a football, and a bunch of girls sunning at the water's edge. I signaled to Clyde that we were getting close.

He nodded and pointed to the beach. Turning to John, I shouted, "He wants to ski ashore. Give him some speed before the drop. Remember to keep an eye out for early breakers."

John gave me a thumbs up and cut toward the shore. He was wide open and closer to the swimmers and the breaking waves than I thought was safe. But it was the only course available.

John yanked the wheel hard to the left, back out to the open water, slamming me into the side of the boat. When I got up off the deck, I saw Clyde heading straight for the beach like a rocket. John had misjudged both velocity and length of runway. Clyde was in what we called a scrape.

He carved through swimmers and over waves as best he could, while bleeding off as much speed as possible in the face of the rapidly approaching shoreline. Once through the swimmers, he leaned back hard. He was slowing, but not nearly enough.

To compound his problems, a late breaker launched him into the air. It was a spectacular show for everyone on shore, but not so good for Clyde. The flight cost him valuable drag needed to slow before the beach. His ski landed in mere inches of water, sticking hard in the sand. Clyde continued on. Coiled tightly in a ball, he tumbled head over heels through the remaining surf and up onto the beach, in a white cloud of sand.

Lying flat on his back for a moment, he sat up, then stood, checking himself for damage at each stage. Everyone who had seen the wipeout burst into laughter and applause when he stood and bowed.

John said, "He seems to be ok."

"Yeah, he's milking it for the girls."

"Smart."

We anchored the boat and swam ashore, dragging our cooler behind. Candice walked up to greet us, but the other girls remained huddled around Clyde, tending to his raspberries and bruises.

"Glad y'all came. Nice show," Candice said as we walked with her toward the girls.

One by one, Carol, Ava, Rhonda, Connie, and Vicky turned to greet us. Candice tapped me on the shoulder and said, "Hey Sam, I want you to meet my cousin."

Turning, I just stood there, spellbound. Her golden hair framed a beautiful, tanned face, with crystal blue eyes, inviting lips, and button nose.

"Sam, this is my cousin Tracy. Tracy, Sam's a friend from high school."

Was my smile goofy? Was I smiling? I couldn't speak.

Tracy's face lit up, "Nice to meet you Sam. That was some entrance you guys made."

Grateful for the lifeline, I grinned and said, "Yeah, those two require constant supervision. It's nice to meet you, Tracy"—

Bill grabbed my shoulder from behind, "Guys, come on." "We need you for a game of volleyball."

John accepted and ran off. I turned back to Tracy and said, "Can we talk later?"

"Sure," she smiled. "Have a great game."

Clyde continued regaling the girls with stories of Cape life as I trotted off. After an hour or so of sand-scraped elbows, knees, and chests, we were happy to call it quits when our female cheering section broke up for lunch. Our banter was more congenial on our walk to the cottage deck than it had been during the game.

Some of the gals had set out sandwich makings, tea, and chips on the picnic table. When Tracy came through the screen door onto the deck, I ran up to her and asked, "Can I join you for lunch?"

"Sure, that'd be great, I'd love to hear more about Cape Lookout. How long have you been coming here?" she asked.

"For as long as I can remember. My earliest memories are staying at the McPherson cottage on the Morehead side of the sound. We started staying on my dad's sailboat about five years ago. He started building it in our back yard. Neighbors got a kick out of asking him when the flood was coming."

Tracy laughed and said, "It must have been pretty big."

"It's a thirty-five-foot motor sailor. When he got as far as he could with the frame, he trucked it to Marshallberg for boatbuilder Ray Davis to finish. She's a beauty and sleeps our family of five."

Freddy shouted over the chatter, "What do you guys want to do after lunch?"

"The waves look perfect for body surfing," I said.

Others in the group agreed and Candice said, "We've got some boogie boards in the garage."

Tracy and I ate a little faster to keep up with the crowd.

"Guess we'll have to catch up on the Cape later. Will you teach me to body surf?"

"I'd love to." *Easy on the eagerness, Sam.*

"Let's hit the beach." Freddie screamed.

Most of the group had finished eating and started moving toward the beach.

"You ready?" I asked Tracy.

"You bet. Let's get out there."

We tossed our plates and cups into the trash, and jogged toward the water, side-by-side.

"Have you ever body surfed?" I asked.

"Years ago, as a kid, but swallowing all that sand and water got old. I quit when I scraped my nose pretty bad."

Seizing the opportunity, I studied her nose and face closely. Surprised by my boldness, I said, "Hmmm, it looks great now – don't see any damage."

She laughed and said, "Good to know Sam, thanks."

She was beautiful *and* sweet – so easy to be with and talk to.

"Take a look at the surf. There are two sandbars out there. The one further out slows the offshore swells and makes them stand up in the shape we like to ride. See it out there?

"Yes."

"Watch the face of the wave, you might see fish in there."

"I think I just did. That's so cool," she shrieked.

"The bar closer in, slows the waves so they fall over, or break. When the tide's high, you can usually ride over the inside bar, but when the tide's low, scrapes can happen. The water level's about right now, so your cute nose is safe."

She smiled and said, "That's good." Her face glimmered in the bright sunlight.

We waded into the surf through the small sudsy breakers until we were about neck high. "Let's start here and work on form. When the wave you want is about ten yards behind you, face the shore, push off hard on the bottom, and swim like crazy. When you feel the wave pushing you, straighten your body and thrust your right arm toward the shore, with your weight on it. Some people put both arms out and fly like Superman, but the preferred form is like swimming, with your left arm by your side to steer and to pull out of the wave when it starts to get shallow."

I demonstrated and Tracy caught on quickly. She looked like a pro in the smaller waves. After a few rides, I asked, "Are you ready to try the bigger ones further out?"

"Yes, let's do it."

She took to them easily, like on the smaller ones. After a few rides, we kicked back and floated for a while, beyond the breakers. Without talking, we just watched the wispy clouds float slowly across the blue sky. A beautiful girl I could barely talk to a few hours ago was floating beside me, totally relaxed, even when we brushed against each other. I was falling for her. She was beautiful, had an awesome body, and was *nice*. Really nice to me. I had to tell her how I felt, but was tongue-tied, just like this morning.

Pull it together Sam. She's nice right? She won't laugh or shame you like those stuck-up cheerleaders. Taking a couple of long, deep breaths, I rolled over, off my back and said softly, "Tracy?"

"Mmm-huh?" Her face and eyes were dazzling in the sunlight reflecting off the water.

"What is it, Sam?"

Encouraged by the kindness in her voice I said, "Tracy . . . I think . . . I think I'm falling for you."

There it was, out there. No getting it back. I was glad.

Her eyes lost a little of their sparkle and she pulled back, ever so slightly, looking pensive. After a few uncomfortable moments, she responded with unexpected tenderness.

"Sam, I like you, a lot, and could easily fall for you. I have a boyfriend. I'm going home tomorrow to pack for a trip out west with him. We're going to work there for the summer.

My heart sank like an anchor.

"—Well, that doesn't surprise me. You're perfect. I hope he knows what a lucky guy he is."

"That's really kind."

"Where is home?"

"Raleigh. Candice invited me to come down about a week ago. I said no initially to get ready for my trip, but she talked me into coming for a couple of days, and here I am.

"Yeah, here you are. Well, I'm glad you came." *Was that true?*

With a big grin she said, "I am too. I wouldn't have met you or learned to bodysurf."

Her joy was irresistible. "How did you decide to go west for the summer?"

"My boyfriend spent a month on a ranch near Yellowstone last year with his family. He fell in love with it. The way he described the beauty and adventures made me want to go. A friend of his dad's, with the Park Service, helped us get jobs at the Yellowstone Lodge. I'm not sure if it's something I'll love, but it sounded like fun."

"Tracy, I love the way you jump at adventure. You are beautiful, athletic, exciting, and most of all, nice. You're different than any girl I've ever met."

"Oh my," she said, "There you go again. We'd better go in before my big head pulls me under."

I forced a smile and started swimming toward the waves' break. We rode together for one last wave. Our walk to the cottage was a quiet one.

Reaching the girls in front of the cottage, Tracy smiled before turning to join them. The guys were in their own group as the radio blasted Dusty Springfield's "I Only Want to Be with You."

Standing between the two groups, I suddenly felt confused and alone, like I didn't belong in either one. Worried that Tracy would notice, I shuffled off to the guys. John was telling a few about his year at VES and how horrible the football season had been, despite his efforts to carry the team.

Rusty jumped in, "While you were away John, we had a horrible year, at Sanford Central. The merger of our two high schools made everybody angry. Blacks had to leave theirs and ours doubled in size. Half our classrooms were in trailers. At least they were air conditioned. There were riots, knife fights, and bathroom brawls. It was a mess until the National Guard came in to settle things down."

"You know," I said, "As bad as it was at first, we learned to live with each other. In a lot of ways high school got better. The football team had its best year in a long time. The band was great, and pep rallies were hilarious. We made new friends."

"Yeah, I suppose you're right. It wasn't all bad," Rusty said.

Clyde leaned in to say, "Let me tell you about making new friends." He had the group's full attention.

"At the beginning of that crazy year, you didn't walk on campus alone. One morning I had to. I was coming back from the principal's office. There'd been a misunderstanding between my English teacher and me about who was supposed to be talking. I figured the safest route was to go by the cafeteria, then through the main building. That path offered the fewest places for ambush.

"Passing the cafeteria, I saw Sam eating alone at this long table near the window. He was right in the middle of the black section. For some crazy reason, I went in and joined him. Three big black dudes walked up, and the biggest one said, 'This is our table. Get out of here, Cracker.'

"Sam looked up at him, then down the long table and said, 'There's plenty of room, why can't we join you?'

"Surprised by the suggestion and Sam's cool, they looked at each other flummoxed. The big guy glared at Sam, gritted his teeth, and clenched his fist like he was about to bust Sam in the mouth."

Clyde looked at each guy in the circle before continuing. He had taken us back to a time and place we wanted to forget, but we were hanging on his every word.

"With a bead of sweat rolling down his face, Sam looked at the big guy, then at the other two and said, 'Guys, what are we doing? You don't want to be here, any more than we do. But it doesn't seem like those in charge are gonna change their minds. Their solution is Army guards. Seems like it's up to us to figure this mess out. Why don't we have some lunch, and get to know each other?'"

"They sat down. Next thing you know, they were talking about what they liked most about their school and we were too. We were all talking at the same time, kidding around, and laughing. By the end of it, we had three new friends, Andre, William, and James."

Stories in the group continued as the wind settled and the sun's light became golden soft. Candice approached and said, "We're going in for showers and will start supper soon. You guys are in charge of grilling the burgers." Looking at John, Clyde, and me, she said, "We'd love for you three to stay for dinner."

We looked at each other and John said, "Burgers sound much better than what we've got for dinner. We'd love to join you. Since we can't add anything, we'll do the cooking and cleanup."

Seeing Tracy walking toward the cottage, I said, "Fellas, I swam all afternoon, so I'm gonna let you handle the cooking duties tonight."

"What you meeeean cousin, is that you spent all afternoon falling for that girl. Tell you what, we'll give you a pass tonight if you cook and clean tomorrow night."

"You've got a deal. Thanks."

A few of us remained behind to bring in the chairs and umbrellas. I pulled a hose from under the deck to wash the salt and sand off them. The moment I turned on the spigot, a blood curdling scream from the right corner of the house pierced the evening calm. Candice burst through the back screen door shouting, "Turn off the hose. Please don't run it until everyone's out of the shower."

Turning the faucet quickly, I called over to say, "Please tell whoever's in the shower that I'm sorry."

Candice grinned and said, "I'm pretty sure it was Tracy."

Nice move Sam.

I reached for a beach towel that was hanging on the deck rail and wiped the salt off my body. A half-full pitcher of water on the picnic table provided a quick shower for my hair and face. Squeezing as much water as I could from my hair, I pulled on my tee shirt that had hung over the deck rail since our morning swim ashore.

five

Impossible Love

The cottage living room was empty. It was still warm from the afternoon, despite the ocean breeze and overhead fan. Dim lamps burned on either end of a shiny avocado-green sofa casting yellow halos on the red pine walls and ceiling. A thin jute rug covered a beach-worth's sand underneath. Behind the door, girls busily readied themselves for the evening. Laughter and muffled conversations blended with whining hair dryers.

I sat on the sofa and flipped through one of the *People* and *Teen* magazines on the coffee table. It fell to the floor when Tracy opened the door looking more magnificent than any of the celebs in that magazine.

Her shiny, golden hair tumbled onto a white linen blouse, immodestly buttoned to follow the contours of her figure. Short, cutoff blue jeans accentuated her tanned, athletic legs.

"Wow. Tracy, you look *magnificent*."

"In this old shirt and jeans?" she playfully protested.

"You'd look great in a canvas sail bag."

To avoid drifting further into peril, I tacked. "I'm sorry for the abrupt change in your shower temp. Who would have guessed the outdoor hose was connected to the shower line?"

She laughed and said, "It's OK, the jolt gave me a second wind. You don't need to apologize. This afternoon was one of the best times I've ever had."

"It was for me too. I wish it didn't have to end."

"So do I," she said with a note of sadness. "Tell me about you. Where are you from? What are you doing this summer?"

"Sure, but let's go to the deck. It's cooler out there, and it'll be crowded in here soon."

"Great. Lead the way."

We walked to the far corner of the empty deck and sat facing each other. The moon was bright, and the air had cooled to a point that the temperature was imperceptible.

"Well, I grew up in Sanford, but my family's spent summers down here for as long as I can remember. My uncle and father built a house out on Cape Lookout, where we're staying this summer. It's about 14 miles that way. Have you ever been out there?"

"No, I grew up going to Wrightsville Beach."

"Watch." I gently turned her toward the Cape. "In a moment you'll see a flash from the tall lighthouse."

"I saw it. That's so cool."

"That's our guide home."

"You mean you are going back tonight? Out there, in the dark?"

"Yeah, it's dark, but that flashing light shows us the way home. It's a fun trip, as long as the weather is good. If it gets bad and we lose the light, we steer 127 degrees on the compass to find the Cape. We might wind up in the North Atlantic if we're off by a few degrees to the south, so we try to avoid bad weather," I said with a smile.

"Our parents let us have the house for the summer if we take care of it. We're supposed to keep it supplied and running smoothly. There are some things we have to do tomorrow.

"It's not all work though. We have great waves for surfing. We ski, sail, race jeeps and jump sand dunes. When those things get old, we come up with new stuff like hood surfing, sand skiing on old car hoods, and skiing in the ocean behind the Jeep. There are no parents and no rules. We can do anything we want, whenever we want."

Tracy's eyes gleamed. "I can't imagine being alone like that."

"It's a big island, but we're not completely alone. There are about ten other cottages on the southern tip of the island with families during the warmer months. We know most of them.

"Sally and Les Moore run a small marina, bait, and tackle store. They live out there year-round. They have no problem filling in for our parents when we screw up. There's also a Coast Guard station if we get into a real jam."

Sitting up straight, she said, "Tell me more about Cape Lookout. It sounds really neat."

"It's the southern end of the North Carolina Outer Banks. The ocean between Cape Hatteras and Cape Lookout is called the 'Graveyard of the Atlantic.' More than 5,000 ships have sunk out there in the last 500 years because of the dangerous shoals, currents, and pirates. You can see some of the wrecks from our house."

Tracy's eyes opened wide. "Is there treasure in them?"

I smiled and said, "Maybe, but it's practically impossible to find. The islands actually move as their sands shift over time with storms and tides. Any treasures have long-since been scattered, buried, or carried away by buccaneers and locals.

"There's an old lifeboat up the beach from the A-Frame, shot full of machine gun holes. They say it came from a freighter that was torpedoed by a German U-Boat before WWII. Their captains were ordered to leave no survivors who could report how they were sunk."

Tracy gasped. "That's horrible."

"It makes me angry to think about it. Merchant ships from here that supplied England during the early months of the war had to use the same narrow straits around the Cape as the old sailing ships. It made them easy targets for German submarines lying in wait. Atlantic Beach old-timers say they could hear the explosions and watch the ships burn on the horizon from their front porches."

"That's horrible," Tracy said.

"A friend of mine knows a salvage diver who just discovered a sunken U-Boat. It's in 125 feet of water, too deep to explore, but we want to dive on it just to see it, maybe even touch it."

"So, you scuba dive?" Tracy asked. "Clyde and I do. We learned last summer in Morehead, from a former Navy Seal. He taught us things that weren't part of the course.

"The toughest challenge for me was when he set an anchor line in 80 feet of water. He tied tanks and respirators every twenty feet down the line. We were supposed to dive, without a tank, find the respirator, clear it of seawater, take a breath, and repeat until we got to the bottom. For proof, he challenged us to bring up a handful of sand."

"That does sound scary" Tracy said, leaning in.

"The scary part is coming. When you dive, water pressure increases and it gets colder as you go down, making it harder to equalize the pressure in your ears and hold your breath. The worst part, on this particular day, was that visibility was zero, halfway down the line. We had to find the last two tanks and regulators in pitch-black darkness. It was terrifying.

"He said the exercise taught us to relax in stressful conditions. It taught *me* to pray. It was Jesus who got me down that line and brought me back.

"I did grab some sand on the bottom, but I put it in my pocket. I wasn't about to give up a good hand in case I needed it to find a tank for another breath."

"Well, that explains why you're so comfortable in the water."

"Maybe. Once you get comfortable breathing underwater, you become part of the environment. The fish practically ignore you. I wish I could show you."

"I do too. Sam," she sighed.

"Do you have a girlfriend?"

Surprised by the earnestness in her voice, I paused to answer thoughtfully. "I dated a girl for a couple of months before the summer. We went to parties and hung out.

Tracy gazed inquisitively into my eyes as I spoke.

"She never felt more than a friend to me, and we didn't have much in common. When we said goodbye for the summer, it was really goodbye. We made no promises to stay in touch or even to pick up where we'd left off. No. I don't have a girlfriend."

Her eyes twinkled in the moonlight.

"Tracy, I hoped this afternoon that I'd found my girlfriend."

"Sam, if we'd met last summer, you would have found her."

"Wow, I, I don't know what to say."

"I will cherish this day, always," she whispered.

I was rolling in a huge wave of emotions. I knew not to fight currents more powerful than I was, but it was hard. It was so unfair. We might be in love now – had we met a year ago. But she loved another, and I couldn't change that. Only she could.

I turned toward the boys at the grill and with a tremor said, "We're supposed to be cooking. I'd better check on the burgers."

As I stood, Tracy took my hand and said, "Please sit with me at dinner, I love hearing your stories."

It took all my strength to smile and say, "I would love that."

At the grill, the boys talked in three huddles. Not up for socializing, I headed into the kitchen to let Candice know the burgers were nearly ready. The room buzzed with girl-talk and food prep. Connie poured a pot of green beans into a large serving bowl and Ava placed steaming ears of corn onto a large platter.

Ava looked my way and said, "Thank you for organizing this afternoon's activities. I tried bodysurfing but wasn't good like Tracy was. You're a good teacher."

"It was all Tracy," I said, turning slightly in retreat. "She's an excellent athlete, easy to teach."

Ava persisted. "She must have been fun to talk to. Y'all were out there a long time. Anything there?

Shaking my head, I said, "No, she has a boyfriend."

"Oh, I'm sorry Sam."

Ava was a good friend. We'd known each other since kindergarten. She was one of the sweetest and most understanding girls in our gang and a good advisor when I had girl problems. I occasionally felt she wanted more from our relationship but didn't feel the same way. Had I been kind enough?

"Thank you, Ava. You're a good friend to me."

Turning toward Candice, I asked, "What can I do to help?"

While opening a bag of chips, she pointed to the corner of the table and said, "Take these trays and condiments and set up the dining room table. We'll serve from there. Let everybody know we'll eat when the burgers come in.

While finishing up the table, Tracy slipped in beside me and whispered, "Remember, you're my dinner date tonight."

There was that feeling again. Had I missed something along the way, or was it just Tracy being Tracy? I smiled with a wink and said, "You bet. I'm with you."

Just then, John burst through the screen door with a huge platter of steaming hot, black-charred burgers. "Dinner's ready," he shouted.

Close behind him were the rest of the grill gang, in varied clusters. When most everyone was in the room, I tapped a glass pitcher for quiet, and gave Candice's serving instructions.

The happy havoc resumed when I finished, and the girls began serving themselves. The guys followed like seagulls attacking a spilled bag of chips on the beach.

It was a fun crowd, unpretentious and caring. We truly enjoyed each other's company. I scanned the room drinking it all in, until Tracy caught my gaze. Her face lit up like a candle. She turned everything I thought I knew about girls upside down.

With a huge grin, I wanted to run over and hug her like I'd never let go, but I walked instead.

Last ones through the line, we collected enough of the picked-over food to fill our plates. Neither of us showed any interest in our selections.

Trays in hand, we walked out onto the crowded deck. Turning toward Tracy, I tilted my head toward the ocean, and she nodded in agreement. When we stepped off the deck, the sand was still warm. A gentle sea breeze tossed curls around her face and shoulders. The beach, ocean, and surf sparkled in the bright moonlight. What a thrill it was walking beside this incredible girl. She made me feel special. She liked me—really liked me—for who I was. She never made me feel less-than.

Approaching the rim of the shore, I said softly, "How about here?"

"This is perfect, perfectly beautiful."

We lowered our trays and ourselves to the sand, sitting very close to each other without saying a word. We just sat there, staring at the shimmering stars and ocean laid out before us. The waves lapped and a warm breeze caressed our faces and bodies. Occasional puffs lifted her blouse exposing her beautifully tanned, and untanned skin. Her warmth radiated over me. We were so close.

In that moment, we turned toward each other with uncertain, but eager anticipation. Her clear blue eyes flashed in the moonlight, and I was rolling in waves of emotion all over again. When her sigh brushed my face, I pulled her close and kissed her. I kissed her like I'd never kissed a girl before. Her firm body melted in my arms. The ocean, the beach, and the stars all began spinning around our own island paradise. I was lost in time and space. I wanted this moment, this place, this everything to last forever. I began to feel dizzy but knew that a breath would end the moment.

Steadying both of us, I looked deeply into her eyes and said, "This has to be enough, enough for me to remember you, and you to remember me."

"Sweet Sam, I won't forget you."

"I hope I haven't hurt you."

"You have not. I don't feel guilty. We shouldn't be together like this, but we are, and I'm glad. We'll find our way back to each other if it's meant to be."

Nodding, I took a deep breath of damp sea air, and swallowed the feelings I wanted to share. I stood and extended my hand to her and said, "It's getting late, and my ability to resist you is exhausted. We'd better join the others."

She stared at the stars and ocean for a time, then at me, seemingly to sear this moment into her memory. She took my hand and stood effortlessly. We lifted our untouched trays and started a slow walk back to the cottage, hand-in-hand, without words.

Everyone on the deck had finished eating and some were cleaning up. As we approached, Candice came up and said, "John told me you guys are going back to the Cape tonight. Can't I talk you into staying here in our living room?"

"Thank you, Candice, you've been great, and we've had a really good time. Most of all, thank you for introducing me to your cousin. She's fantastic and I hope we meet again," forcing a smile. "We have a full day's work tomorrow. It's an hour's ride home and the moon sets shortly. We'd better get started."

Gathering our stuff, we said our goodbyes to the guys and kissed the girls. Tracy and I embraced noticeably longer and tighter than the others, and it was lost on no one.

We walked into the breakers, still dimly lit by the setting moon, and dived in for a swim back to the boat. Once aboard, Clyde pulled up the anchor, John started the engine, and I settled into the stern for the long, dark ocean ride home. Clyde and John shouted and waved goodbyes and the crowd enthusiastically answered.

Tracy stood motionless – apart from the group. As we pulled away, she lifted a hand to her lips. She held it there for a few seconds, then released a kiss. Clyde and John saw it but turned away and said nothing.

When we sped up, the crowd turned to make their way back to the cottage. Tracy stayed behind. Her eyes were fixed on me and mine on her. Gripping the stern to steady myself, I squinted fiercely to watch her diminishing figure until darkness pulled her from my sight.

When the few remaining lights of Atlantic Beach faded below the horizon, the sea and sky turned black as ink. The damp salty wind buffeting my face, the rolling waves, and the engine's drone offered none of the excitement they had this morning.

John steered for the lighthouse. Clyde was beside him for company and another pair of eyes to scan the black expanse ahead of us. I remained in the stern, feeling lost in an infinity of black sea and sky. Why come so close to love – only to lose her? The wind, the gentle rolling of the boat, and the drone of the engine lulled me to sleep.

six

Maintenance

I regained consciousness in a heap on the deck with a stinging forehead. The engine whined as it blasted water and sand on me. Struggling to find a handhold to lift myself, I realized my shoulder was numb.

"What happened?" I mumbled when the engine stopped.

"Captain Courageous here, ran us aground, wide open," Clyde snapped.

"Sorry, I couldn't see the buoys without a flashlight, but was sure I was in the channel. Y'all OK?"

When I made it to my feet to list my complaints, I was awestruck. The night was amazingly still. It seemed we'd landed on another planet. A whisper of warm breeze suggested Earth, but not like I'd ever seen it. The velvety-black sky was close enough to touch, but it was also infinite. There were layers upon layers of sparkling stars, some large, some small, some bright, some clustered, but every single one of them was crystal clear. The Milky Way was more spectacular than ever. Stars filled every bit of sky, and more. The black water of the sound around us was like glass – perfectly mirroring every detail of the starry heavens above. We were in a star globe. No one dared utter a peep, in awe of God's majesty.

Without warning, the bright sweeping lighthouse's beam shattered our trance and star globe. Following a couple more sweeps, Clyde shouted, "We have our flashlight. Watch the beam travel across the water. There. There's a buoy. There's another one."

Using Clyde's rotating 'flashlight,' we methodically mapped our channel. Soon after, the rising tide began to right, then lifted our boat. After thirty minutes of stargazing and swatting mosquitoes, we had enough water under us to walk our way to the closest channel buoy.

Having no desire to repeat our mistake, we watched every sweep of the light before striking out for the next buoy. One by one, we made our way to the dock. The grounding had added another hour to our painful trip home.

Walking down the dock toward the Jeep, John said, "Ain't that just like the Cape?"

"Yeah," Clyde growled, "but I wish she'd been a bitch some other night."

I agreed, any other night would have been better. When we got back to the A-Frame, we fell straight into bed, salt, bruises, bug-bites, and all.

Hours later, when I noticed the stars through my porthole beginning to fade, I gave up trying to sleep and slipped quietly out of bed. I grabbed my pants and snuck out of the room to avoid waking the others. I needed time alone – without the banter.

It was dark and still when I stepped onto the back deck. The sand and sea grass sparkled with each sweep of the lighthouse's beam. When I walked around the side wall of the house, a cool sea breeze caressed my bare skin.

Falling into the front corner of the wraparound bench, I just sat there, staring out at the ocean, in the direction of Atlantic Beach. The hypnotic breeze and soft light of sunrise carried me back to Tracy's sweet embrace and kiss. I wanted to remember every small detail of her – her scent, her voice, her breath, her touch, her eyes, her body. But already—maybe for lack of sleep, or a bang on the head—the fine details were becoming like shifting sand. My memory of her was beginning to fade, along with my consciousness. Heartbroken, I drifted off.

Sweat rolled down my back and a growling stomach, ignored since lunch yesterday, woke me. Shaking my head to clear the fog reminded me of the bump

I'd received earlier. Hoping some cereal would improve my spirits and headache, I ambled off to the kitchen.

After a second bowl, Clyde and John rumbled down the stairs.

"You're up early, Sam. Lovesick?" John asked wryly.

"Yes, but she's got a boyfriend. They're going to spend the summer out west working."

"Oh man, that sucks, I'm sorry."

"Yeah, I've never felt like this before. I thought she could be the one."

They sat quietly as they poured their cereal, milk, and sugar. After a few bites Clyde perked up and said, "Don't worry brother, she's not the only starfish in the sea. Another one'll come along."

"Yeah, but starfish don't swim very fast."

After a pause, I asked, "What do y'all want to do today? Walter comes tomorrow around two o'clock, if I'm right about your mom's instructions. We need to have everything ready for him, including a full drum of diesel fuel for the bulldozer."

"Man, I can't wait for his biscuits. And his red-eye gravy," Clyde exclaimed.

"Yeah, Walter's biscuits don't have grease streaks in them like yours do," John cracked. "Maybe wash your hands next time."

"Up yours, John. As I recall, you ate every one of 'em."

"Yeah, they were OK. The grit was good polish for my teeth. The flatbed's not running very well and probably needs new plugs and air filter."

"Yeah," Clyde agreed, "The points are corroded, but they'll be like new with some sanding. We can get new plugs and filters in town. I'll get a list of parts together for the generator, Jeep, and flatbed."

"I'll check on the well pump. It hasn't run since last fall and will need priming for sure," John said.

Abundant water was another luxury we enjoyed at the A-Frame. Dad said they had to drill 200 feet to get fresh water, but we felt strongly that they should have kept drilling. The smell of our water, particularly in the shower, was worse than rotten eggs. Dad said the powerful odor and taste came from sulfur, iron, lime, and countless other minerals. We became accustomed to it in time and found that the sulfur cleared our acne miraculously and made our hair grow really fast.

Bringing 300 gallons of water to the surface and then another fifty feet to tanks on the third floor required a high amperage electric pump. It was powered by a large, cantankerous Army generator. The pump required priming after long periods of sitting dry. It was housed in a concrete block house behind the Jeep shed. The duty of priming it almost always resulted in cuts, bruises, and fending off a colony of dark, moisture-loving creepy crawlers. Clyde and I avoided it like no other, happily trading all other jobs. John seemed to revel in the fight.

"I'll get the generator started," Clyde said proudly. John, you can't bully her like you do. She needs sweet talkin'."

"Well, you sweet-talk the damn thing all you want. I'm gonna show that water pump who's boss."

"I'll do the house stuff then. Only two of the propane wall lanterns worked last night. The mantles need to be replaced. We've got enough to go around, but we'd better get some more when we go into town. If y'all get the tanks filled, I'll check the toilet innards. Cape water eats 'em up fast."

"Check out the bottom oven burner too." John said. "Mom told me it was too rusty to heat well. I saw a new one on the shelf over the workbench. It should just slide right in."

"That's a good one John," I said, "Nothing just slides in around here. I'll probably have to cut it out. What time do we want to head out for Morehead?"

Clyde reached for the tide table at the end of the counter and asked, "What's today?

"It's Monday, June the fifth," John replied, slightly annoyed.

"High tide's at ten-thirty this morning," Clyde said. "Can we be ready by then?"

We agreed and went to the shed to get started. On the way, I said, "I'll top off the bulldozer to get as much fuel out of the drum as possible."

We used a hand pump to pull fuel out of their drums. It looked like an old-fashioned eggbeater and was much harder to turn. The dozer sat behind the shed, well beyond the reach of the fuel hose. It took up to ten trips to fill its voluminous tank with a 5-gallon jerry can.

When we finished our projects, we threw down some sandwiches and Check Colas before heading back to the shed. I helped John load the near-empty diesel drum onto the flatbed, while Clyde finished with the engine.

"Sam, kick the starter," Clyde said eagerly.

The motor started quickly and ran much smoother than before. Clyde yelled, "She'll purr really nice when I get the new plugs in her."

I nodded, thinking it sounded just fine with the old ones. John finished tying down the drum and hopped on. I put her in first and idled out of the shed using the motor and clutch to slow our descent. Brakes were another short-lived auto component in the harsh conditions of the Cape. When we started down the ramp, the drum slammed hard into the seats with a loud crash.

"Nice job, John," Clyde shouted.

"John failed his knot-tying badge in Scouts," I yelled.

We gave the ribbing a rest when he growled more seriously than usual.

Roads on the island were little more than deep tire tracks in sandy valleys between dunes. Some were covered by grass, but most were sand. A vehicle practically steered itself once the tires were in the tracks. We didn't often get stuck, but when we did, it was the guy behind the wheel who hiked back to the A-Frame to get the Jeep, with its working 4-wheel drive.

Loading the diesel drum was easier than we thought it would be because the tide had lifted the boat enough to roll it right in. We were quickly on our way.

It was an exceptionally hot day with little wind. When we got up to speed in the boat, the moving air was welcome. Settling into the stern seat I became aware, once again, of how tired I was from my sleepless night. Leaning back, I stared at the few wispy clouds in an otherwise clear blue sky. The drone of the outboard and blast of cool air mesmerized me into a sleepless dream.

There I sat, in the cockpit of my Cessna 150 airplane on the runway, engine running and ready for takeoff on my first solo flight. It was on a Saturday morning, not too long after I had gotten my driver's license. Clyde and two of my friends had ridden to the airport to watch and cheer me on. I remember wondering, was I scared to death or excited beyond my wits? Either way, I was glad my friends were with me.

Pushing the throttle full in, I began rolling. At 65 knots, I pulled back on the yoke and was airborne – all alone for the first time. My instructor had encouraged me to do some sightseeing while aloft, so I headed for my house to see what it looked like from the air. After a couple of circles around the neighborhood, I turned toward the municipal tennis courts and the Elks Club pool. Most of the cute girls I knew would be there. If I wasn't a good enough tennis player to get their attention, this would sure do the trick.

Traveling along Weatherspoon Street, to Horner, then to Carthage, I spotted the tennis courts and dropped down for a closer look. There were kids everywhere. When a few looked up, I swung around and gave a wing-wave. With "Grazing in the Grass," blasting on the plane radio, my maneuver was more exaggerated than intended. A quick check of my altimeter confirmed I hadn't dropped below the regulatory minimum of 500 feet. It would have been a shame to lose my certificate before I even got it.

I throttled up and pulled back on the yoke to gain some altitude before heading back to the airport. Here I was, flying all by myself, with clear blue skies and the green trees and small buildings of my hometown below. Everything felt perfect. Then, out of nowhere, came this sinister voice in my head, "Man can't fly—you can't fly."

Terror shot through me, temporarily blinding me in a flash of bright white light. I gasped for a breath, shook my head, and cried out, "Lord, help me."

My vision returned as a strange warmth washed over me. Looking around, I saw that I was still flying – mostly straight and level. I corrected and went through my checklist. Airspeed – good, vertical speed – good, rpms – good, altitude – good. I was in a cold sweat and shaking, but my body was answering commands. I thanked God for pulling me back from the edge of panic and started looking for the airport. "Southeast Sam, the airport is southeast of town."

Airport in sight, I felt my heart rate and breathing begin to return to something closer to normal. I checked the radio frequency and reached for the microphone. Taking a deep breath to project an audible voice, I said, "Sanford Municipal tower, this is Cessna 793 Whisky Foxtrot requesting permission to land."

Permission and information obtained, I said a prayer and did my best to shake off the jitters. On my downwind leg, the sight of Clyde, Lynn, and Johnny on the tarmac waving gave me the final boost of confidence I needed.

When the runway flattened out, I pulled back on the yoke, to flare enough to stall the plane and touchdown gently onto the runway. Flaring a little higher than intended, my landing was more of a planting. But I was down, and I was alive! Even though I had done the maneuver dozens of times with my instructor, that one was completely different – terrifying and exciting in one hot moment.

Exhilarated, I slowed the engine, braked hard to make the next exit, and picked up the mic to ask for taxi instructions.

My instructor responded, "Congratulations Sam, good to have you back. Taxi up to the office. We have a little ceremony for you."

Now this little *ceremony* went back to the days of tandem flight trainers, before the technology of airplane intercoms. The instructor communicated with his student by tugging on his shirt tail. Having just completed my first solo flight, my instructor was going to cut off my shirt tail as a right of passage. He was going to signal to the world that I no longer needed my instructor to fly an airplane.

Wiping the sweat from my face as I pulled up to the office, I killed the engine, and locked the brakes. It was the happiest moment of my life when I opened my door and saw the guys running toward me yelling and fist pumping.

Clyde was first. "Well done, Sam! Man, you planted that plane, but good."

Lynn and Johnny laughingly agreed. Enjoying the happy support of my friends, I nodded and joined in the laughter. My instructor nudged his way into the gaggle to say, "Excuse me fellows, there's one more thing Sam needs to do today. Pull your shirt tail out young man and turn around."

"Must have been pretty hot up there," he said. You might appreciate a little extra ventilation. We'll need to let this thing dry out before we can write your name and date on it for the airport wall."

Hearing those scissors cut was an indescribably proud moment.

I did it!

Later I came to realize that my efforts had been much less for the love of flying than for the challenge of doing something big, and scary. Part of it was to impress my Uncle Charlie. He had flown in the Pacific during WWII. But when I shared my accomplishment with him later that afternoon, he took little notice. Maybe it was a bad day for him, but it hurt me deeply. Why was it so important for me to impress him? My dad made a big deal over my accomplishment, but Uncle Charlie's recognition had eluded me, yet again.

The slamming of the near-empty diesel drum into the side of the Whirlwind woke me. John was running wide open through the S-turns. Clyde yelled, "Don't baby her, John."

Looking across the sound toward Harkers, I thought about our trip to Morehead. It would be easy to pop over the bridge to Atlantic Beach and see Tracy. But it was already after noon. She'd surely be on the road by now – back to him.

Pulling into the marina, I glimpsed my Mustang in the hotel parking lot. The newness of having my own great-looking car hadn't lost its shine one bit in the last three months. Even though mom had owned the car for five years before me, and I had driven her very hard on the farm for many of those years, she felt new to me.

After a quick tie up at the dock, we ran to the Mustang, cranked windows down and turned up the radio. Off we went with The Who singing "I Can See for Miles." Traffic was light on the Island Road, and we made good time on Highway 101 through Beaufort into Morehead City.

After picking up parts and oil at Kittrell's Auto, we headed for Cheek's Hardware in downtown Morehead. The store was a time capsule from the 1920's. The creaking, oily wooden floors, the whir of large ceiling and standing fans, and the smells of rubber, fertilizers, seeds, cardboard, and dust hadn't changed in half a century. It was stuffed full of the usual hardware supplies. But there was a shelf, close to the ceiling, that wrapped all the way around the store. On this shelf were the most curious instruments, contraptions, and small appliances from a long-gone era.

The moment we placed our lantern mantles and insect repellant onto the counter, a large parrot in the corner, squawked, "Cash or charge - cash or charge?"

Laughing, John said, "That will be charge please to the Charles Reeves account."

On the way out of the store we ran into Bud Doughton. He and John had been at VES together.

"Hey John," Bud called.

"Hello, Bud. What are you up to this summer?"

"I'm mating for Cap'n Josiah Bailey on the *Diamond City*." She was a 40-foot sailboat ferry that transported day-trippers from Harkers Island to the Cape. "It's a great way to meet girls," Bud said.

"Now that's thinking." I broke in. "If you get any time off, join us at the A-Frame for some surfing and skiing."

"Thanks, that sounds great. I'll leave a note on Mr. Credle's message board when I know my schedule."

Back at the marina Mr. Credle told us to circle around to the fuel dock after we'd loaded the propane tanks from Mr. Teel. He'd help us fuel up the diesel drum. We rock-paper-scissored to see who would sit in the hot sun pumping diesel for 30 minutes. John and Clyde congratulated me and headed into the store for some ice cream.

Sitting on the side of the boat pumping fuel, the painfully slow advance of the meter allowed plenty of time for people watching. The marina was full of folks enjoying their vacations. A couple of fishermen walked by with a cooler, presumably full of fish. A cute teen walking from the motel started me wondering – would I ever meet a girl as perfect as Tracy? Hearing a motor coming behind me, I turned to see a family entering the marina in their boat with a couple of well-tanned teen girls in bikinis.

Suddenly, smelly diesel fuel began running over the top of the drum. Releasing the lever, I looked around to see if anyone had noticed. Putting the hose and nozzle back into the pump, I grabbed a rag off the top and sopped up the spill.

Our ride back to the Cape was fast and easy. On the way, John suggested that because it was low tide, we might wait until tomorrow morning to unload the heavy drum. We usually went to Les and Sally's to use Les' davit (crane) to raise it from the boat. But low tide doubled the distance to lift the 400-pound barrel with the rusty old hand-cranked wench.

We figured there was just enough daylight to wrap up the most important projects, like servicing the generator, pumping the water, and hooking up the new propane tanks. Clyde started with the generator. I connected the six full propane tanks to the bank of twelve. We used only six at the time, allowing the other side to be removed and refilled.

John growled as he grabbed a wrench and a bucket of water before heading around back of the shed to tackle the pump and the demon-possessed building that contained it. Seconds later obscenities blasted through the shed wall.

"Guess the pump house got the first round," Clyde said as he continued working on the generator. A few minutes later, about the time I'd finished with the propane tanks, Clyde patted the instrument panel and in a syrupy voice said, "OK sweetheart, show me some love."

Pressing the starter button, the engine turned over, slowly at first. The oil-soaked floor planks began to vibrate under our feet as the monster machine thundered to a start. It soon settled down to an idle, much smoother than I'd remembered. Clyde beamed and I gave him two thumbs up, with no chance of being heard. He let it run for a minute or so, then turned it off to recheck the oil.

Just then, John came through the shed doors with a few battle scrapes and cuts and said, "It's primed and ready to go. Let's give it a try."

"Great job, John," Clyde said, pressing the ignition button on the generator. Just as before, she fired right up, and the electrical output gages quickly turned green. When Clyde flipped on the pump switch, the engine's pitch lowered an octave under the strain, but the circuits held, as shown by the green panel.

I ran up to the third-floor tanks to listen for water. Hearing splashes, I yelled from the back stairs, "Good work John. She's pumping."

Back in the shed, I asked, "You guys want to do some Jeep skiing after the tanks are full?" Clyde jumped up and said, "Hey, that's a great idea."

I yelled, "I'm first," before he could get it out.

We swept and straightened up while we waited for the water tanks to fill. I so enjoyed being in the shed. It was a warm and cozy place in the cold months and a cool one in the summer, when the generator wasn't running. It was like a barn for machines. We took care of them, and they took care of us. Working on machines didn't come naturally for me like it did for Clyde and John. But I loved being with them, watching, taking part in their work, and joining in their triumphs. It was a great place for us to work things out.

"Kill the generator and the pump," John called out to Clyde when he saw the overflow pipe shooting water from the top of the roof.

As we jumped in with our ski gear, John fired up the Jeep and threw it in 4-wheel drive to drive up the large dune beside the house and back down toward the sound. When we reached the water's edge, I jumped out with the ski and ski rope handle. Wading into the calm water, I gazed westward at the golden afternoon sun, setting over Atlantic Beach. It was the same sun that had gone down on Tracy and me just twenty-four hours before. It seemed a lifetime ago. I tried to replay every moment of the day, the night, the embrace, the kiss, and the goodbye. I was dazzled by the bright sparkles on the ocean.

John's shout jerked me back to reality. On my signal, I was yanked out of my blues. I began making turns in the shallow water. The ski's fin occasionally shirred in the sand, but not enough to stick and cause a wipeout. In case of a fall in inches of water, it was best to land on the back. A back sanding was better than face and chest sanding, we thought.

There was almost a mile's run inside the curve between the A-Frame and Les and Sally's marina, but a large shipwreck lay about halfway between us, forcing a stop and a 180. It was a good place to change skiers. After we each had a turn, we headed back in the near-dark for some long overdue showers. There was nothing quite like the clean you felt after washing off encrusted salt and grime. That shower-fresh feeling at the Cape was especially unique.

Exhausted from the day, nobody wanted anything more than sandwiches. The radio was tuned to the top-40 hits station WMBL, which stood for *Where Morehead and Beaufort Link*. Beach Music was their specialty in the evenings.

The DJ played some great records and told stories about how the bands and songs came to be. We played cards and listened late into the night to the Drifters, Catalinas, Barbara Lewis, Big Joe Turner, Little Anthony, and the Embers. So many of the lyrics reminded me of sweet Tracy. Did she think of me?

Around eleven-thirty, the DJ's stories stopped. His intros became slurred and nonsensical. Pauses between songs grew longer. Then, after Paul Mauriat's "Love is Blue," finished playing, there was dead silence. A cool breeze whistling through the porthole screens and the boiling whir of the propane lanterns were the only noises we heard.

"There wasn't even a 'Star Spangled Banner,' or a see ya," Clyde said.

We'd put our cards down and listened for any signs of life. Then it came. Starting as a faint rumble, then louder, and louder.

"The old coot's passed out," Clyde howled. "He's snoring right into the microphone."

We resumed our game after a good laugh. A few minutes later, we heard the studio door open. There was some shuffling and then, "Dad, Dad, wake up." The mic went silent and a few moments later, "Love is Blue" played again.

At the end of the record the younger man we'd heard earlier came on and said, "We apologize for the interruption in our programming. Guess the last song was just a little too mellow for the old fellow. Thanks for staying with us. This next song was written for the musical *Hair*. This group has taken it to the number one spot on the Billboard Top 40. Here's 'Aquarius,' by The Fifth Dimension."

Clyde said, "This is my last hand fellas, I'm calling it a night."

Noticing a grimace when he touched his thigh, I said, "What's the matter with your leg?"

"I think the cut I got on the beach yesterday's infected." He turned in his chair to show us a bright red boil.

"Wow," John said, "that looks pretty bad. I saw some activity at the Barden cottage this afternoon. We'd better have him check it out."

"That's a good idea," I agreed. Looks like the redness is spreading. Let's get some antiseptic on it tonight and head over first thing in the morning."

"OK," Clyde said.

I pulled the first aid kit from the cabinet and gave Clyde a tube of Mycitracin to rub on it. We ambled off to bed and were soon asleep.

seven

Dr. and Mrs. Barden

The bedroom was warm when we began to stir, suggesting we'd overslept.

"Guys, it's eight-thirty," I said. "We've gotta get to the Barden's before he takes off. How's your leg feel this morning, Clyde?"

"It hurts."

"Let's get going then," I said. "With any luck, Mrs. Barden will make us some of her famous blueberry pancakes."

The Barden cottage was halfway between Sally and Les' house and the Coast Guard Station. It sat on a lush salt marsh about 100 yards from the water. Dr. Barden was a New Bern pediatrician. He and his wife, Mary, had two children, Maryann, my age, and Graham III, Clyde's age. Our families were close through our long association at the Cape and later, in New Bern.

Graham and Clyde had become good friends last year. During hurricane season, Dad had moved his sailboat from Morehead City to the Trent River Yacht Club, which was close to the Barden's New Bern home. Graham introduced Clyde to two of his friends, who had similar appetites for adventure. They spent hours in their small boats racing up and down the Trent River. One morning, they were running three boats side-by-side, wide open, toward a swing bridge. Graham yelled out, "Don't worry, we do this all the time!"

Do what all the time? I wondered. The answer came moments later when Graham and Hubie closed in on either side of us – close enough to occasionally bump. We were going through the bridge three abreast – full speed.

When we neared the opening, I breathed a little easier when I saw that we had a good twelve inches on either side of our three boats. What was I worried about?

Graham was an extremely clever and resourceful guy. He helped his dad maintain a large bank of marine batteries and solar panels used for lighting the cottage. Their lights weren't as bright as those at the A-Frame, but they required no gasoline or propane.

Maryann was my age and great-looking. By the time I realized it, she had acquired a team of admirers from high school.

Pulling into the driveway we saw doors and windows open but no other activity. Just then, Dr. Barden burst through the kitchen screen door and gave us a big wave.

"Come on in boys. It's great to see you."

Dr. Barden was a large, jovial man. His wife, Mary, was his perfect mate. She enjoyed Cape life as much as he did. She was a fine cook and made everybody feel welcome. We never left their house, on the Cape or in New Bern, without a full stomach and some new stories.

We said our hellos and shook his hand as we filed through the screen door into the kitchen.

"Welcome to the Cape," John said. "We saw you arrive yesterday."

"Yes, Mary and I came ahead to open the house up before the weekend. Maryann's coming with some of her friends and Graham will be here too."

"Great, it will be good to see her. Hello Mrs. Barden," I said as we entered the cozy, well-stocked kitchen, smelling of bacon, pancakes, and propane.

Standing over a large griddle, she turned full round, with a huge smile, spatula in hand and said, "Hello boys, can I interest you in some blueberry pancakes? Bardie and I found the most beautiful berries at the Garner Farms stand on the way down."

"We don't want to impose, but we had sort of hoped," John said eagerly.

Clyde and I promptly agreed and thanked her.

"Have a seat boys," Dr. Barden said motioning his hand around the large kitchen table.

In no time at all, Mrs. Barden laid a plate in the middle of the table. It was full of steaming hot pancakes stuffed full of oozing hot blueberries.

"Dig in and tell me those aren't the best blueberries you've ever tasted," she said proudly.

"The best pancakes too, Mrs. Barden," I said. "We're going to Harkers later today and would be happy to pick up anything you need."

"That's very kind, she said. I'll take a look and let you know."

Quickly downing half of my stack, I asked, "Dr. Barden, what's the connection between your family and Barden's Inlet?"

"Well, my dad grew up down here fishing, out of Mrs. Harker's Inn. He knew most of the locals and became familiar with their concerns. A big problem for them was that in 1934 a hurricane closed the channel that had given them quick access to the ocean. The closure forced them to motor or row fifteen miles to the Beaufort Inlet to get to the offshore fishing grounds, then back.

"When my dad was elected to Congress, one of the first things he did was pass a bill that directed the Army Corps of Engineers to dredge a permanent channel from Back Sound to the Bight, creating what is now Barden's Inlet. It is said some Islanders named their babies after him."

"That is so cool," Clyde said, while scratching his leg.

"What do you have there, Clyde?" Dr. Barden asked.

"It's the reason we came to see you. We thought it might be infected and wanted you to take a look at it."

"There's no question. We've got to lance this one. You boys finish your breakfast and I'll be right back."

Clyde's face turned ashen as he pushed his plate away. John and I grabbed the last two pancakes from the center, poured on the syrup, and gulped them down, ahead of the pending operation.

Setting a tray of gauze and medicine on the table, Dr. Barden moved in beside Mrs. Barden to heat a single edged razor blade on a stove burner.

Just then John said, "Dr. Barden, my dad says this house sat beside the lighthouse as the light keeper's home."

Clyde relaxed a little with John's distraction.

"When Mary and I got married, Sam Whitehurst, my dad's law partner, gave us this lot as a wedding present. He'd gotten it from a client he did some legal work for out here. I later learned that the Coast Guard was accepting bids for the chief lighthouse keeper's quarters. I won the bid and hired a fellow named Jimmy Collins from New Bern to move the house.

"There were some power lines blocking the way, so Jimmy asked permission from the chief to drop them. When he was told that permission would have to come from Washington, Jimmy went ahead and cut them, moved the house, and put them back up.

"Later that afternoon as the house was being lowered onto its new foundation here, Jimmy returned to the Coast Guard station to learn from the chief that Washington had denied his request.

"Jimmy said 'Chief, I'm awful sorry, but I've already moved the house.' Pointing out the window, he said, 'She's settling onto her new foundation right now. I was so sure the government wouldn't mind if we dropped the lines to get that house off their property—like they wanted—I went ahead and cut the line, moved the house, and reconnected it. Do you think they want me to put the house back?'"

When Clyde laughed, Dr. Barden made a quick incision, and the worst was over. A little squeezing, dabbing, antiseptic and bandage made for a quick, painless procedure.

"There you go Clyde. How does that feel now?"

"Thank you, Dr. Barden, it's already a lot better."

"Keep it out of the water for a few days and let it heal. Apply some of this ointment two or three times a day."

"We won't have much time for water activities anyway. Walter is coming this afternoon for a couple of days to help us with some projects."

"Oh, that's wonderful. Please tell him we said hello."

eight

Walter

Walter Martin was a gentle giant of a man. He was Uncle Charlie's farm manager, but he was *our* farm-father. He taught us how to fix tractors, mend fences, pull up stumps, bail hay, and slaughter pigs. But most of all, he showed us how to be joyful and kind, by the way he lived.

Walter, and his wife Cleo, had nine kids. We played together but drifted apart in our teens for no good reason. I never felt our relationships were strained by the racial issues outside the farm. Sure, I remember, as a kid, asking my parents why there were 'Colored' bathrooms and water fountains. They tried hard to answer in ways I might understand.

Mom and Dad were clear voices in the community for racial equality and desegregation. They spoke plainly to us about the evils and hurts caused by segregation, but my personal experience with Black people came from years of playing with Walter's kids on the farm, isolated from the issues that mom and dad talked about.

My innocence was lost in '66, when the violence of desegregation invaded my middle school and later, my high school life. I even felt drawn toward hate when friends were sent to the hospital with cuts and concussions from battles on the playground and in the courtyard.

I was blessed to be positively influenced by people I loved and trusted. Their explanations of the reasons Blacks felt the way they did made a lot more sense to me than the ideas shouted by some of the angrier, more vocal white and black kids at school. Walter was one of those men who stood in the gap. He chose to see the good in people. Despite the despicable treatment he'd endured in his life, he always demonstrated remarkable restraint.

He put up with a lot of patience-testing from us kids too, but he never lost his temper, at least in a violent way. He and John had a father-son love and playfulness that often involved Clyde and me. Some of our interactions were pure play, happy contradictions to racial tensions outside. Others provided life lessons on manhood.

Walter had remarkable strength. He stood six feet tall and weighed some 240 pounds – all of it muscle. There were countless stories all over town of his muscular feats.

One morning when he was picking up some parts at the International Harvester dealership in town, a couple of high school guys, sitting on the hood of a tractor, called to get his attention. "Walter, we'll bet five bucks you can't pick this tractor up."

With his gleaming bright smile, Walter walked over, grabbed the front, and lifted it a foot off the ground, with the two of them flailing frantically to stay on. When he returned it to the ground, he said, "Fellas, that'll be five dollars – Each."

Following a quick exchange of funds between the two, Walter was ten dollars richer for his effort.

On the way back to the A-Frame from the Barden's, we discussed our last-minute preparations before Walter's arrival. We decided it would be easier if he helped us get the diesel drum out of the boat when we got back to the Cape. After straightening the shed and house, we left for Harkers. From there we took a quick trip to Best's Grocery to stock up on milk, eggs, and flour for Walter's arrival.

When we got back to the marina and went into the store, Mr. Credle was finishing up with a couple of motel guests. Pulling some ice cream from the freezer, we gathered around the counter when the couple walked out.

"Walter's due in any time," John said.

"Wonderful," Mr. Credle said. "It's been months since I've seen him. Guess he doesn't need to come so often, now that you guys are doing all the maintenance, huh?"

"We still need him for the big jobs," John said. "He's coming to fix the bulldozer and teach us how to run it to keep Dad's landing field in good shape."

"Walter's a jack-of-all-trades. I was impressed by his skills during the construction of the house," Mr. Credle said.

The screen door popped open, and there he was, with that giant smile of his. "Hello boys. Mr. Credle, how are you?"

Mr. Credle said, "The boys were just saying what a good teacher you are."

His through-the-nose laugh filled the room, "Well, I've got a lot to teach them this time."

"How was your trip?" Mr. Credle asked.

"No problems at all. Boys, there're a few things in the truck. Take it around to the boat and get it all loaded."

"Yessir," we said, filing out the screen door. When John saw the truck, he said, "*A few things*? Looks like he brought the whole tool shed."

We hopped into the pickup with John in the driver's seat and pulled around to the back, as close to the boat as we could get. Climbing into the truck bed, John lifted one of the boxes labeled 'Dozer Tread.' "Man, this thing's gotta weigh fifty pounds," as he dropped it into Clyde's waiting hands. The box went straight to the ground.

"Dammit John. Thanks for the warning."

Oblivious to Clyde's complaint, John continued with his inventory. "Guess this tool's for tightening the bulldozer track."

When we'd moved all the supplies and coolers into the boat, we parked the truck and went back around to the marina store to let Walter know we were ready.

Now there were few subjects on which our whole family agreed, but on this point, there was 100% consensus. Walter Martin feared the water more than Superman feared kryptonite. To make his boarding as comfortable as possible, we had tied the boat as close to the dock as we could get it. Fortunately, the tide was perfect to lay the gunnel level with the dock.

Walter was in his customary white shirt, mid-blue long cotton pants, and beige straw fedora. He walked slowly and deliberately right down the center of the dock checking for loose boards.

As he neared the boat, John said, "Hop aboard, Walter."

Walter's eyes widened, "There won't be any hopping, John," he responded in a deep, firm voice. He slowly lowered himself to the corner of the dock, keeping his weight behind him. We had heard Dad, Terry, and David tell stories of Walter's water fears. But to actually see him, hear, and feel the terror that so haunted him, was something else again. He looked like he was staring over the edge, of a bottomless abyss.

"Clyde! Hand me a couple of those life jackets," Walter ordered. Taking them together, he slid both of them up his thick left arm. There was no way even the largest jacket would go around him. He repeated the same on his right arm.

Not daring even a snicker, we watched each other's reactions as he slowly placed his feet on the deck and shifted his weight into the boat. When he was sure it would not capsize, he took a firm grip on the gunnel, released the dock, and lowered himself—ever so carefully—into the bench at the stern.

"Walter, you good?" John asked.

"Yeah, let's get this over with, and John, you take it easy."

"Yessir," John replied. But there was something about his tone, or body language, or John just being John, that suggested he would do otherwise.

Clyde and I cleared the lines from the pilings and John idled out of the slip. Once out of the marina and in the open water, John turned back and said, "Walter, I'm going to speed up now to get on a plane."

Walter nodded without a word, as his fingers tightened on the wooden bench like they'd leave dents. His body stiffened like a bronze statue.

With a roar and a cloud of smoke, the Whirlwind labored to cruising speed. The wind was light, and the water was smooth for an easy ride for our uneasy guest. After a few minutes Walter relaxed, and the bronze man returned to flesh.

"You picked a beautiful day to come," I said loudly, looking his way.

"It's mighty pretty out here, but there's too much water."

"Once we're across the sound, it gets shallow enough in most places to walk to the Cape."

"That's what Terry and David always say, but I'm not about to try it."

"Well, it's bright and the tide's high, so there's little danger of running aground, even with John driving."

A hint of terror returned with my reminder.

Clyde asked, "What do you have planned for us?"

"Mr. Reeves wants his runway smooth and packed. The bulldozer's needed for that, so I'm going to teach you boys how to fix it, run it, and *not* break it," laughing big enough to forget where he was.

Clyde and Walter got along especially well. Walter appreciated his eagerness to learn and the questions he asked, but most of all – I think – it was because Clyde made him laugh.

When we came to the S-turns in the shallows, John bumped the throttle to full speed. He had that look – the one that always tightened my gut. His turns were exaggerated through the sticks. He was going fast enough that the heavy boxes slid from side to side. Clyde and I struggled to stay put, holding tightly onto the gunnels.

Walter's eyes opened wide, and he shouted. "John, what are you doing? Stop that!" He roared like a bear.

John was laughing so hard he nearly lost control. When he slowed and looked back at Walter, feedback was fast and clear.

"John Reeves, you'd best not let me catch you when we get on dry land. I'm not kidding you, boy."

John managed a weak chuckle and turned to resume a more reasonable speed. There was very little conversation after that moment, for the remainder of the trip.

Approaching the dock, John called back. "I'll run the boat ashore to unload the heavy stuff."

"Good idea," Clyde said.

The moment we heard sand on the boat's keel, John jumped overboard and ran like his tail was on fire. Clyde and I went over the sides and swung the boat around, parallel to shore. John just stood there, beside the flatbed, wondering what the bear he'd just poked was going to do.

Into the tension Clyde said, "This is as close as we can get the boat Walter. I don't even think you'll get wet."

With the four life preservers still on his arms, Walter climbed over the gunnel and onto shore. Feet firmly planted on *terre sandy*, he removed the preservers, two-at-a-time and tossed them into the boat. Turning toward John, he just stood there and glared.

"I'm sorry Walter. I shouldn't have done that," John said sheepishly.

"No, you shouldn't have, John. But today, I'll let you live."

With a collective sigh of relief, we all returned to the job ahead. John, delighted for his stay of execution, backed the flatbed down to the boat. Clyde and I began handing the gear off and John and Walter loaded it onto the truck.

When he came to the long-handled tool, Clyde asked, "Walter, what is this thing?"

"It's a bulldozer track tensioner. Some of the treads need to be replaced. That's what's in the heavy boxes."

When the boat was emptied of all but the drum of diesel fuel, Walter, sensing our unease, hopped into the boat, and said, "Step aside boys. Let a man show you how to handle a load like this."

We quickly stepped aside to give *the man*, all the room he needed. He addressed the drum like a gladiator sizing up his opponent. Filling his barrel-sized chest with the fresh sea air, in one fluid motion he turned the 400-pound can on its side, jerked it up onto the gunnel, and rolled it off into the shallow water. The deck popped and cracked under his feet, but it held.

We looked at each other like we'd seen a miracle. Heck, it *was* a miracle and I'm positive that in that moment, John was thanking God that Walter was a forgiving man.

"Wow Walter, you made that look light. I bet you could lift all three of us at the same time," Clyde exclaimed.

"If you boys behave, I won't have to," laughing as he caught his breath. "The Lord blessed me with strength ever since I was your age. Always want to use it for good."

Climbing out of the boat, he jerked the drum from the shallow water and rolled it onto the truck bed. It sank by a foot under the heavy load.

"Come on boys, let's get to the house. It's hot out here and getting close to supper time," Walter said.

Now Walter's cooking was legendary. I began to hope that we might get another miracle today.

"What are you planning for dinner?" Clyde asked, eager with anticipation.

"Mrs. Reeves said you boys probably haven't had a good meal since you got here, so I'm going to make you some fried chicken, fresh green beans, corn, and biscuits."

There it was – our second miracle, in as many minutes. In fact, it could be argued that Walter's fried chicken and his biscuits qualified as individual miracles.

"What the heck are we waiting for?" John hopped into the boat and lowered the motor as Clyde, and I pushed it off. Once we had it tied up, we jumped onto the truck and headed home. The flatbed's motor pounded, and the wheels dug into the sand under the heavy load, but she got us home as always.

John backed the flatbed into the shed, and we quickly went about unloading. When the drum was all that remained, Walter tilted it over, rolled it to the back of the bed, and with a grunt, lowered it to the solid plank floor. He grabbed the cooler and said, "You boys straighten up in here and I'll go get supper started."

Stopping by the hose at the bottom of the back stairs, he took off his hat and ran some cold water over his neck, head, and face. After wiping away the excess water, he pulled his ever-ready handkerchief from his back pocket and patted dry.

There were plenty of towels in the bathrooms just inside the door, and Walter knew that. But I couldn't remember ever seeing him use one. Was he so accustomed to the rules of separate "Coloreds" and "Whites" that he followed them even here?" Was it respect? Whatever it was, I was sad that he felt he needed to.

We stacked the tools and boxes, filled the water tanks, and went into the house. Clyde and John headed for the showers first, and I walked into the kitchen and sat down at the counter to spend some time with Walter.

Flour, salt, pepper, and a few spices covered much of the counter. Walter was methodically turning pieces of chicken in the powder. His giant hands made them look tiny.

"How have you boys been getting along out here? Looks like you've got everything running well."

"Clyde's a great mechanic and John's not too bad either, but they're different. Clyde's a tapper, John's a banger," I said chuckling.

Walter laughed. "I know that's right. Here," he said, pushing a bowl in my direction. "Snap the ends off these beans while you're sitting there. Not too much though, 'bout a quarter of an inch."

For a while, the only sounds were those of breeze whistling through the port-hole screens, beans snapping, and chicken plopping in the batter.

"Walter, I'm really sorry about Dr. King's murder and what's going on with blacks and whites."

"I got fightin' mad when Dr. King got shot. I was angry at all white people for a long while, every one of you. It took a lot of praying and time, but the Lord teaches me to forgive, and he helps me." Walter moved the bowl of battered chicken near the stove.

"Mr. Reeves and I made a pact that neither of us would join a group that hated the other. We've gotten along pretty well, your uncle and me. Your daddy and me too."

Stunned to hear this side of a man that I'd never seen angered, I just sat there for a while, snapping beans.

Pushing the finished bowl toward the stove, I said, "You know Walter, we had a really hard time with integration in high school this past year. Black and white kids were hateful toward each other and angry at the system for wrecking our schools. But after a few months, I started making some new friends when I took a risk and reached out. It was really easy once we started talking to each other."

"I'm real glad to hear that. We got a long way to go, but if we talk and listen to each other, and don't let hateful people drive us apart, maybe we can figure out how to live together."

"Just then, John bumped through the bathroom door. Walter pointed to the brown paper sack and said, "Now that you're all shiny clean, you and Clyde take that corn to the back porch and shuck it. Make sure you get all of the silk out. Don't want to be pulling any of that out of my teeth tonight."

By now, Walter had started pounding out the dough for his famous biscuits. He rolled it to an even thickness and began cutting circles with a small jelly jar. The same hands that had just precisely placed a 400-pound drum of diesel fuel in the shed, now arranged small disks of dough in neat rows on a liberally greased pan. Sitting in the rich amber light of a warm summer sun setting over the Atlantic, I thought, more than that man's strength and ability, it was his joy and peace that I admired most.

"Dinner will be ready in twenty minutes if you want to get a shower," he said.

Our two days spent with Walter were uniquely special. He schooled us in the operation and care of the large bulldozer, and we kidded around as we always did. Different though, were his talks on how we should treat people, especially girls, with respect. He got real serious when he said, if he ever heard we were messing up on respect, he would come down on us something like a bulldozer.

As much as we enjoyed our freedom on the Cape, the days we spent with Walter were among the best of our summer.

nine

Provisioning

Our parents didn't visit often, but when they did, Cape life changed – a lot. Preparing for their arrival, we spent days cleaning, sweeping, bed-making, shopping, hauling, and ensuring that every convenience in the A-Frame worked as expected. Our parents insisted on it. On their arrival, our duties became something like those of resort hotel staff. We carried luggage, helped with meals, got fresh seafood, and assisted their beach and water activities.

The upside was that we ate a lot better. We enjoyed the stories of Uncle Charlie's buying thousands of acres on the island in the 50s and early 60s. We thrilled at the adventurous tales of Dad, Walter, Terry, David, and their friends building the A-Frame. They were colorful family stories that we rarely heard anywhere else. Our parents seemed so happy and relaxed on this island.

We wouldn't admit it, but we were each excited they were coming. Our independent island life was fun, but it carried lots of responsibility. We realized early on that the duties of keeping the place running weren't nearly as much fun as we thought they'd be.

Chewing a bite of cereal, John said, "We'd better get to Harkers Island early to start on Mom's list. She said she'd send it to Mr. Credle."

"The Jeep and the flatbed need tuning, but they're OK for now," Clyde added.

"Yea, they'll keep," John said. "Who's gonna notice if they miss a beat every now and again?"

Clyde snapped, "You should have more respect for a perfectly tuned engine. A smooth-running engine is much less likely to leave you stranded John."

"OK Clyde – I'll show more respect for the machines." John laughed.

The song on the radio stopped. "We interrupt our regular programming for this important news bulletin from the South China Sea. Seventy-four U.S. sailors were killed when their destroyer, the USS *Frank E. Evans* was sliced in half by the Australian aircraft carrier *Melbourne* during NATO maneuvers off the coast of South Vietnam."

Looking at each other in astonishment, Clyde said, "That same thing happened to President Kennedy's *PT 109* when it was cut in half by a Japanese destroyer. Why in the hell are we over there? Nobody wants to be. Two of my friends have brothers that just got drafted."

John said, "Yeah, Mom told me David got his letter."

"John." Clyde blasted, "Why in the hell didn't you tell us?"

Vietnam became real in that moment. What had been an interruption in TV or radio programming, was suddenly, deeply personal. David was a favorite cousin. He was cool. He was an ATO at Carolina, a pilot, and he paid attention to us. Our older cousins were too busy being young adults to pay us much attention.

Kenny Rogers' "Ruby, Don't Take Your Love to Town" played in the background. I hadn't paid much attention to the lyrics of that song before, but they hit home this time. The song was about a disabled Vietnam vet whose girl goes to town looking for love he couldn't give her. Nobody coming back from Vietnam, dead or alive, was appreciated for their sacrifice. It was an ugly war, both at home and abroad. There wasn't any glory in it like WWII had for our dads.

With cereal finished and eager to lift the mood, we took off for Harkers Island to begin gathering supplies for our parents' visit. The still morning air made for calm water. The trip went quickly.

Hill's Marina was busy with fishing boats going out and a long line of cars and trailers waiting on the ramp to launch. In the marina office, Mr. Credle leaned around the crowd at the counter to say, "Hello boys. You've got a letter here from Sarah."

John reached for the envelope, tore off an edge, and pulled out the contents. His jaw dropped as he began assessing the extent of our assignment on the multi-paged list. Clyde and I sank along with him as he flipped through the pages.

Noting our reaction, Mr. Credle said, "John, let me take a look at that. It's intimidating, but doable. You boys need a plan. I suggest you start in Straits, at Mrs. Willis' stand. She has the fruits and vegetables you need. She'll give you a good price if you tell her I sent you and that I'll cover your bill on my next visit."

"Can I get a pack of Marlboro please?" A fisherman at the counter asked.

"On your way back from Straits, stop at Best's Grocery and ask for Billy. He'll supply your meat and groceries. And you can get fresh shrimp from us the day you need it."

When the crowd filed out of the store, Mr. Credle said, "You'll need something bigger than that sports car of yours to carry all this. Take the Green Machine," referring to his 1960 Chevrolet CarryAll.

With a huge grin, I said, "Wow, thank you, Mr. Credle. I don't think we could get along without you."

His eyes gleamed. "I'm sure you could, but it would be too painful to watch."

Looking me squarely in the eye as he pulled the keys from his pocket, he said, "This old work wagon's no sports car. She's tired and the marina depends on her. Treat her with respect."

Doubtless of his sincerity, I said, "Yessir, Mr. Credle, I'll treat her like a lady."

His smile returned and he handed me the key. "Get out of here, you wharf rats, you've got a lot of work to do."

Straits was only a couple of miles beyond the Island bridge. Just as Mr. Credle had said, the sign for Mrs. Willis's Fruit and Vegetable Stand appeared moments after turning onto Straits Road.

The shade under the roof was welcome relief from the morning heat. Each bare-footed step across the peanut shell-covered floor calmed and welcomed us in. Bins of brightly colored fruits and vegetables with their sweet and savory aromas overwhelmed the senses. Quiet conversations in Down-East brogue suggested a reverence that we'd unwittingly fallen into ourselves, like we'd walked into a library. This was a distinctly local place, and we felt welcome.

Mrs. Willis introduced herself and with a friendly smile she asked, "How can we help you?"

"Hello Mrs. Willis," I said. Mr. Credle told us you could help us with this list. We've got a large crowd coming this weekend looking for the best fresh fruits and vegetables available."

"Well boys, you've come to the right place," she beamed, as she waved her hands over the array of colorful produce. While scanning the list, she called to a pretty young brunette at the back of the stand. "Cynthia, bring a couple of carts and some boxes, please."

John whispered into Clyde's ear, "This trip's looking better already."

"Down boy, Clyde whispered. "She looks too young for *me*. I know she's too young for you," Clyde snickered.

I was sure John hadn't heard Clyde's warning over the noisy wheels turning in his head.

As she approached with the carts, Mrs. Willis introduced her saying, "Boys, this is my daughter, Cynthia."

Clyde and I greeted her, and John followed, clumsily formal. "It is a pleasure to meet you Cynthia, I'm John."

She pushed the carts and boxes toward her mom and said, "Hello John, guys."

Mrs. Willis walked off to begin filling the boxes.

"Do you live on the island?" John asked.

"Yes," she answered, "just up the road."

Angling for her age, John continued, "I guess you go to East Carteret High then?"

"Next year," she answered.

"What do you do when you aren't working?"

"I love to ski and surf, and just hang out with friends on the boat."

"That sounds like us," John responded. "How often do you get out to the Cape?"

"Whenever mom doesn't need me here."

"Well, stop by the A-Frame next time. We're probably close by if there's a blue boat at the dock near the lighthouse."

She nodded with a smile and said, 'Maybe we will."

Mrs. Willis, from a few isles, called over, "I'm making good progress on your list. Mr. Credle has your shrimp, but we've got fresh clams if you need them."

"I wish we could get them from you," Clyde said, "but our aunt insists that we rake them at the Cape the day she makes her chowder."

I agreed. "I don't think we can get out of that."

Mrs. Willis smiled and said, "Your aunt is wise. Clams harvested yourself are the best." We nodded politely as if we agreed.

Placing a large basket of peaches into the last cardboard box, Mrs. Willis said, "That's it boys. Your list is complete."

"Thank you so much, Mrs. Willis. Can Mr. Credle pay the bill when you see him next?" I asked.

"Of course," she said with a smile. "We enjoy his visits several times a week."

We loaded six large boxes of fruits and vegetables into the back of the blazing hot Green Machine. The midday sun had super-heated it after we'd rolled the windows up to keep the dust of the parking lot out.

We piled in, careful to keep bare legs off the skillet-hot vinyl seats and quickly rolled down the windows. In the light traffic, I sped up to get some breeze blowing through the truck. We pulled into the parking lot of Best Grocery minutes later.

The air-conditioned store was a feast for the body and eyes. Ads for colas, beer, cigarettes, and sunscreen with their hand-painted price signs filled the walls. Groceries, neatly arranged on the shiny chrome-lined shelves ran down long narrow aisles of mirror-like green floors. Colors vibrated under the bright florescent lights and neon wall signs. Our progress through the store was marked by the smells of produce, groceries, tobacco, coffees, all floating on that wonderfully chilled air.

We headed toward the back of the store under the sign 'Fresh Meats.' A large, jovial man standing behind the counter said in as thick a Harker's brogue as we'd ever heard, "What can we do for you boys today?"

"Mr. Credle told us to talk to Billy Best for help with our shopping list," John said holding up the well-wrinkled pages.

"Well, you've got him. You boys sure do talk funny. I don't believe you're from around here, are you? But if Mr. Credle sent you, you've gotta be good people."

"Our parents are Charles Reeves and Sam Bass from Sanford," John said.

"Oh yes," Billy said, "I've met Mr. Bass. Nice fellow. He's tryin' to get us Islanders to join him in the negotiations with the State before the Park Service takes over. He and your uncle seem to want to do the right thing, but most folks around here aren't so sure. The newspapers don't help their case."

"Uncle Charlie says the newspapers don't ever call to get their side of things," I said. "My dad says the state's going to win, eventually, and turn the Cape over to the federal government for a National Seashore. He just wants to make sure the locals can keep fishing, hunting, and camping, like they always have."

"You tell your daddy to come by and see me. I think maybe I can get some more folks to help," Billy said.

I nodded enthusiastically, "Thanks Mr. Best, that'd be great. They're coming this weekend with some friends, and we're hoping you can help us get ready for them."

Billy took the list and scanned it quickly. "We can help you with all of this," he said proudly.

"We've got some coolers in the car." Clyde said.

"OK, bring 'em in and we'll get started."

When we returned, Billy began throwing blocks of ice into the two large ones. He wrapped huge cuts of meat into plastic bags, threw them into the cooler, then poured on some shaved ice. Finished with the meats, he came around the counter and began filling them with butter, milk, cheeses, and eggs. While he did that, we filled boxes with flour, cornmeal, and other dry goods.

"Take these coolers to your truck and I'll total up what you've got in your boxes. I expect you want to put all this on Mr. Reeves' account?" Mr. Best asked.

"Yessir, please," John answered. "Would you mind adding three drinks, Mr. Best?"

"Help yourselves to the drink cooler boys. They're on the house."

"Thanks Mr. Best." Clyde turned to say. "I can see why everybody calls your store Billy Bestie's."

He smiled ear to ear and crowed, "That's a might kind of you, young man. We do what we can to please."

Back at the marina, we transferred our load quickly and returned the keys to Mr. Credle, with hearty thanks. Our trip back to the Cape was fast and easy in the high and calm water. We'd decided we'd beach the boat and back the flatbed to the water's edge for fast unloading. John and I swung the boat in as shallow as we could get it and Clyde backed the flatbed down.

My yell for "Stop," to Clyde, was a little too late. The wheels sank to their axles. "Pull up a little."

Clyde gave it some gas, but the tires spun freely. The vehicle sat motionless at the water's edge. John and I pushed against the wooden bed with all we had, as Clyde struggled in vain to find traction.

"Hold it," John yelled, grabbing a couple of planks from the truck bed, handing one to me. After digging a trench in front of the back wheels, we each jammed our boards under the tires and tried again. With a little rocking and forcing the boards further under the tires, the truck eventually struggled free of the wet, sandy trap.

We immediately began loading the boxes and coolers onto the truck. After securing the Whirlwind, we headed for the house and started unloading and storing our large haul from the day.

When I came to the tenderloin, I said, "Hey, why don't we carve off three steaks for supper?"

John sighed and said, "Nah, we'd better not. We don't want to start off in trouble."

"Guess you're right," I said, "We'll have a couple of my famous Chef Boyardee Pizzas instead. I roll the best thin crust on the island."

John chuckled, "Sounds great, I'm starved."

"Your mom's letter said they were flying in with Senator Staton and his wife tomorrow, and you know how your dad loves to surprise us early. Mom and Dad sail in on the *Quintet* with the Lawrences and Howards tomorrow afternoon. Things'll really get crazy then," I said excitedly.

After dinner we sat around the poker table, played a few hands, and shared a few stories of the past school year. Clyde was having a good night with the cards and seemed especially annoyed when John called it a night.

Clyde and I remained at the table. I started a game of solitaire when Clyde said something out of the blue. "I wish I was smarter in school like you and John.

Guys gave me a real hard time last year. The thought of going back to Central next year scares me to death."

"What? You're the life of the party, Clyde. You've got a great bunch of friends who love motors and cars like you do.

—I'm sorry. I didn't mean to blow off what you just said. I know you've had a rough time in school these last few years. Mom and Dad are doing the best they can to figure out what's right for you."

"Like military school? I hated it there. It was awful."

"I know that was a big mistake. I heard Mom and Dad talking one night about how unhappy you were, and what they could do about it. The experts didn't seem to have any answers either. I know one thing – they surely won't send you away again."

"Yeah," Clyde said, "but I hate Sanford. I like it down here a lot better."

"Yeah, I do too, but I don't see how that would work with the family living three hours away in Sanford. Mom and Dad will figure something out. I know it."

"Thanks Sam, I appreciate you listening. I know Mom and Dad are trying. I just wish they didn't have to. I wish I was smarter."

"Alright. That's enough. You're a genius with your hands and you have a memory like an elephant. Everybody loves to be around you. Don't you notice how people crowd around when you start telling your stories? I wish I could make people laugh like you do. I'm jealous."

He smiled at the notion that his older brother was jealous of him. "To tell the kinds of stories I do Sam, you'd have to make them up. My stories are real. They come from my own crazy life, and everybody loves stories about crazy-ass people."

I laughed and said, "Crazy or not Clyde, people love you and your stories. You tell them better than anybody I know. It's a gift that makes you friends wherever you go."

"Thanks, Sam," he said with a crack in his voice.

"God made you just right, brother. Do you remember when we were at Camp Don Lee, and you got so homesick? They moved you into my cabin because you couldn't get over it. Do you remember what we talked about when you first came?"

"Yeah, we talked about Jesus," Clyde said.

"Yes. Our counselors had reminded us that Jesus was always with us—when we needed him or just wanted to talk to him—all we had to do was pray. We prayed that afternoon. You had a great time after that. You became the star of my cabin."

This sounds like a good time to pray. Now let's hit the sack."

ten

The Parents - Reeves

Puffs of wind whistled through the porthole screens, a motorboat hummed across the bight, and an occasional gull screamed. But it was brighter, and warmer than usual. Reaching for my watch, I was startled to see that it was almost nine. We had a lot of cleaning and straightening left to do before the first wave of parents arrived.

I went through the list in my head as I pulled on my pants and shirt. Then, faintly at first, I heard the unmistakable drone of a twin-engine airplane approaching. Before I could wake the others, the roar was deafening. My top sheet flew off and was pulled almost through the porthole by the vacuum created by a plane whizzing just feet over the roof.

"Oh no, it's Uncle Charlie," I screamed.

Clyde and John sat upright in their beds, faces frozen in terror. "We aren't ready, what the hell are we going to do?" John screamed.

In an unusually commanding voice, Clyde said, "Let's draw to see who picks them up while the other two clean up, really fast."

We circled fists for a quick rock-paper-scissors. John's paper covered my rock, and my rock broke Clyde's scissors, electing him as our pickup man.

The list was long and would require smart, fast work, but it was Clyde in the hot seat. His job was to slow-walk the pickup and return of Uncle Charlie, Aunt Sarah, Senator Bill Staton, and his wife, Ellen. They were four highly intelligent, driven people, who did not suffer inefficiency or incompetence.

With a sneer, Clyde slipped on his pants and shirt and walking out to the back steps said, "I'll do my best to slow things down, but you guys have a lot to do."

John and I flew downstairs and began straightening, sweeping, washing, and starting the generator to fill the water tanks. We had done so well getting supplies ready, we hated to spoil it with a messy house for them to walk into.

"Why did we leave so much to do?" John growled as he burst through the back screen door heading for the shed to start the generator and water pumping.

As I swept, straightened, and washed dishes, I thought about the differences between the two groups coming, mostly about my uncle and mom. Charlie was Mom's brother, but they were so different. He was a force – large, emphatic, and assured. Mom was demure, graceful, and winsome. He was seven years older and had been in college and New York during Mom's adolescence. He loved her dearly and she loved him, but not in a hugging kind of way.

Moments later, John called from the back deck to say the flatbed was headed our way. I joined him to greet our arriving guests. Clyde drove up the clanking steel-matted driveway carefully to avoid bouncing his passengers. We said our hellos and assisted them down from the flatbed. Sarah directed the Statons into the bathrooms on either side of the back hall to freshen up. Charlie went straight into the living room as we started unloading the bags.

When I passed the kitchen, Sarah asked me to chip some ice from one of the large blocks in the coolers along the wall. She put a pot of water on the stove for iced tea. "Boys, you've done a good job getting ready for us. Looks like we have everything we need."

John said, "Thank you, Mother, we had some good help from Mr. Credle, Billy Best, and Mrs. Willis in Straits."

Lighting one of his big green cigars, Charlie called from the sitting area, "I've got a job for you boys. The driveway needs regrading, and the Marston mats need to be straightened and reconnected."

"Yessir, we will," I said. "Uncle Charlie, where did those mats come from? They look like the ones on airstrips in war movies."

"That's right. The Seabees, the Navy Construction Battalion, used them to build landing strips on islands in the South Pacific as we captured them from the Japanese. We had to land fighters on them fast to defend against enemy bombers that were always close by. They got their name 'Marston Mats' from their testing at Mackall Airfield in Marston, North Carolina."

"That's so cool," Clyde said. "Don't worry, we'll smooth out the drive while y'all are away from the house. It'll be noisy straightening the bent ones."

Charlie said, "Thank you Clyde, don't bother fixing the bent ones. There should be some new ones in the dozer shed."

As the Statons walked through the kitchen, Sarah called out, "Iced tea and lemonade will be ready soon. Anyone want something in the meantime? We have various soft drinks, canned fruit juices, and tap water. The water's an acquired taste."

"I'd love a cola," Ellen said, and the Senator agreed. Bill Staton was the family attorney, but he was also a state Senator overseeing the condemnation of land for the state.

"Clyde, please wash your hands and help me squeeze some lemons," Aunt Sarah said in a hurried voice.

"Yes, ma'am," Clyde answered.

From the living room, Charlie called, "John, would you go into our room and fetch the long white tube off our bed, please?"

Turning toward Bill and Ellen, he said, "I received the architect's concept drawing of the Cape Lookout Club just before we left this morning."

Receiving the tube from John, Charlie removed the plans and rolled them out onto the large round coffee table. Senator Staton and I placed seashell ashtrays on the corners to hold them flat.

Waving a hand across the page, Charlie said, "You are the first to see the future Cape Lookout Club. The central lodge and hotel are here. The residences are scattered around the property, all interconnected by these covered board-walks. The buildings are designed to blend into the natural surroundings of dunes and grass. Electric golf carts will be used for transportation, like those on Bald Head Island.

"Charlie, this is an amazing plan," Senator Staton said. "It will significantly boost the property's value for our case. Do you have the capital and financing lined up for the development?"

"We are far enough along that the bank will provide letters of intent when we need them."

"Excellent," Senator Staton said as he studied the drawings.

Looking west, I saw a couple of sails on the horizon, but couldn't tell if they were the *Quintet*. I'd keep an eye on them.

John asked, "When will you start this project, Dad?"

"Well son, let's just say we aren't in a big hurry, but we'd like to have the permits to show we're serious."

Sarah, who had joined the group said, "Ice cold lemonade is ready. Any takers?"

"Yes ma'am," I blurted, before our guests could answer. Thankfully, no one else spoke up.

I walked out onto the front porch to take a better look at the approaching sailboat. It was the *Quintet*, and they were making good time. I went back into the kitchen. "Aunt Sarah, all three of us will need to go pick up Mom and Dad's crowd. They'll be here in about 30 minutes. Is there anything we can help you with before then?"

"Thank you, Sam," she replied. "This corn needs to be shucked and beans snapped. We're having steak tonight. Did you get the charcoal?"

"It's in the shed. I'll put a bag and lighter fluid by the grill."

Clyde and John started on the vegetables, and I headed for the shed. On returning, Sarah asked me to chip some ice into a small, clean cooler for the cocktail hour. It was clearly understood that we should not run out of ice during this time.

By now the *Quintet* was entering the mouth of the bight. I saw that there were six sailors aboard – my parents, the Howards, and the Lawrences. The tranquility of the A-Frame was about to go from library quiet to class-change chaos.

"Let's head for the dock guys," I said. "We can help them tie up."

We hurried out the door, excited for the arrival of this rowdy, happy crowd. Clyde and I hopped into the flatbed. John headed for the shed and Jeep. Moments later we were racing toward the boat basin.

eleven

The Parents - Bass

At the first opening between the dunes, I spotted the *Quintet*, under full sail. They would arrive at the boat basin soon after us. Dad had built the basin last summer as a shelter against the strong currents and wave action. It had begun to fill with sand, but there was still enough water to navigate at low tide.

When we climbed up to the deck level and could be seen over the basin wall, Dad called from across the water with his deep booming voice, "Hello, boys!" Everyone else aboard waved and shouted hellos.

Dad steered the sailboat into the wind and gave the order to drop the sails. Bill, Paul, Isabel, and Mom went to work lowering and furling the jib, main and mizzen sails. Clyde, John, and I nodded at each other, impressed. As they finished, Dad headed into the basin and shouted, "Stand by the dock lines."

The current and wind proved no match for his skill in powering the *Quintet* into the basin. Bill and Paul were ready on either side to fend off, if needed, but it wasn't necessary. Isabel was on the bow with a dock line in hand. She tossed the windward line to Clyde, and he walked it forward, guiding the boat into her berth. I took the port stern line from Mom and made it fast. Isabel tossed the starboard bow line to John. Paul used the boathook to add a spring line on the port side to keep her off the dock at high tide when the other lines loosened.

"That was a very impressive landing. Y'all looked great coming in." John said. "Mom, Dad and the Statons got in this morning and are at the house now."

Bill Lawrence yelled from the bow, "Are you boys having a good time out here?"

"The best," Clyde shouted.

Dr. Howard joined in with a chuckle, "Well it doesn't look like you've been overeating."

"We've worked our butts off getting ready for your visit," Clyde cracked with a smile.

As the boat eased downwind toward the wall and deck, Dad spotted an object that threatened to damage the boat. It was a diving board we'd nailed to the deck a few days earlier to practice our flips. Scrambling toward it, he yelled, "What in the hell is this doing here?"

He reached over and ripped it off effortlessly – with its dozen nails – and threw it onto the dock. Eyes wide open, Clyde spoke up to say, "Sorry Dad, that was our diving board."

"OK, just think next time."

"Yessir," we said together.

Dad was six feet four inches and tipped the scale at around 250 pounds. He had a closely cropped beard and a fully shaved head that made him look like a bearded Mr. Clean. His tanned, shirtless torso was cut with large, well-defined muscles. Contrary to his intimidating appearance, he was a kind and thoughtful man. Dad had a broad range of interests and talents that included banjo, guitar, singing, painting, acting, and people – most of all, people. Conversation was perhaps his greatest interest.

He was the kind of dad boys wanted and needed. He played catch, helped me carve pinewood derby cars for scouts, disciplined when I deserved it, challenged me to try new things, and most of all, respected my choices. He was present when I needed him and supportive when I wanted independence. He never talked much about God. He had been in the church choir, but not anymore.

As much as Dad loved the middle of the action, Mom was happy on the sidelines. She was a good sport to endure Dad's late nights' singing and change-the-world conversations. Boating, Cape Lookout, and midnight debates really weren't her thing.

At 43, Mom retained the beauty of her youth. Time had passed her kindly. Her softly curled brunette hair framed clear blue eyes and a classic face. She held a regal bearing, even when handing off the mooring line of a sailboat.

Most of all, it was her kindness that charmed all who met her. She had a delightful sense of humor, but as far as I can remember, never landed a punch line well. It was her infectious laughter at the end that made her jokes so endearing.

Mom and Dad's boat mates were the closest of friends. They were like a devoted family to each other. Mom and Isabel were second cousins and close like sisters since the cradle.

Isabel and Bill carried on like smitten teenagers. Mom had said they married shortly after high school. Izzy would do anything for her Bill, and he would walk across hot coals for his Izzy. Bill was a large man, like Dad. He had a defining goatee, laughter, and gregarious demeanor that reminded me of Burl Ives' Santa Claus cartoon character. It was impossible to remain unhappy around that man.

Nan and Paul were more reserved, but just as lovably devoted to each other and the group. Nan was closest to mom in personality and charm. Paul was an MD and the group's wise guy. He rarely let a point go unchallenged. And he had the wits required to hold a position, whether or not it squared with his own. Despite his slight build, he loved riling up the heavyweights in a spirited debate.

Perhaps his medical mind provided him with an advantage in knowing where a person's buttons were. I think needling was his way of taking your temperature, so to speak.

Handing a bag to Clyde, Bill asked, "How 'ya doing, boy? Y'all staying out of trouble out here?"

"Yessir, you bet." Clyde answered. "Did you have a good sail out?"

"It was beautiful," Isabel chimed in gleefully. "We made it in record time." The two of them seemed to enjoy outdoing each other in spreading cheer. They were my favorite couple.

"Looking forward to your cooking, Izzy," Clyde said.

"Don't you worry." Isabel said with a big smile. "We're going to get some good hot food in you boys."

"Dad, the basin's infilled some more, but I think you'll have two or three feet below the keel at low tide.

He nodded and said, "Thank you son, I was afraid we didn't get those retaining walls down far enough. This current's so strong through this inlet here that the sand moves several feet below the surface."

Clyde and John loaded the last bags onto the vehicles while everyone made their way from the boat to the Jeep.

"Everybody, find a place and we'll be on our way shortly," Clyde said. With Dad last to hop on, and an "All aboard," he and John reached for the starters and engines fired up. We began lumbering our way through the deep sand toward the A-Frame. Our rowdy crowd hung onto their luggage, to each other, and laughed and yelled over the roar. How great, I thought, to have friends like these, enjoying everything together, and willing to do anything for each other.

Conversations continued as they headed into the house. Bill's voice carried over the rest as they cheerfully greeted Sarah, Charlie and the Statons.

"Sarah," Bill crowed, "you look totally relaxed already. This island agrees with you. Ellen, I can see you're easing into Cape life too. What do you boys have over there?" he asked Charlie and Bill.

Dad, Paul, and Bill walked into the living room and Senator Staton said, "These are Charlie and Sam's plans for developing the new Cape Lookout Beach Club."

Charlie began like a school kid, anxious to present his show-and-tell, uncharacteristically animated. He guided the group through the plan, building-by-building. Dad moved closer, eager to see it for the first time.

"Owners and members will be able to dock their boats in a protected deepwater marina. The clubhouse, restaurant, and sundries store are here. There will also be a swimming pool and tennis courts. The villas will be on stilts, above storm tides. They are designed to have minimal physical and visual impact on the land. Boardwalks will be raised as well."

Isabel said "Charlie, these plans look almost unbelievable. Do you really think you can make this happen?"

Charlie answered, "We can absolutely make it happen, but only when the Outer Banks Seashore Park Commission lets us know how much land they need for a State or National Park. Then the Carteret County Board of Commissioners needs to rule on whether to allow us to proceed. If the state decides to take all of our land, these plans give us the leverage we will need to negotiate a higher price than an undeveloped desert island would bring."

In the last few weeks, I had grown an intimate, even spiritual relationship, with this place. How sad it would be to lose it so soon – like Tracy.

Senator Staton added "The National Park has already been authorized by Congress and signed by President Johnson. Governor Bob Scott wants to accelerate the state's purchases of land here and correspondence from them has increased."

Charlie added, "The state has spent five years, so far, dragging their feet. So, we decided to begin our own development in case the park falls through. Another possibility in the process, suggested by Governor Sanford, is that the state may not need all of our land. Either way, these drawings and permits will be useful."

Dad said, "If we do develop, it will only be on a small portion of the Cape. We want to make sure that locals can continue using the Cape and Core Banks as they always have. The Park Service sometimes goes too far in restricting access, in the name of conservation. We are working with locals to get protection for them written into the charter with the National Park Service.

"Part of why we favor the federal government taking over most of the Outer Banks is that they will build up the dunes and stop development like has occurred on the northern banks of Hatteras. Permanent buildings expose the island to inlets caused by hurricanes. Breaches could flood the brackish waters of Currituck Sound with seawater, damaging the farming and fishing of eastern North Carolina."

Sarah called from the kitchen, "Boys, I'm going to need at least a bushel of fresh clams tonight. Can you manage that this afternoon?"

"Yes ma'am." Clyde answered. "The tide looks perfect now."

We headed for the shed, threw some clam rakes and a trashcan into the back of the Jeep and drove to the boat. We knew at least a dozen places to get clams within a mile of the A-Frame, but all required the boat.

Jumping into the driver's seat, Clyde said, "On the way back from Harkers yesterday, I noticed a ton of clam holes in the shallows just before Barden's Inlet."

"Man, I can't wait for Aunt Sarah's clam chowder," I said. "It's the best ever, and I've had a lot of it in seafood restaurants." We all agreed.

Clyde's hunch quickly proved correct when our rakes immediately clinked when we sank them into the sand. Each pull brought up three, five, even more fist-sized clams. With little effort, we quickly filled our can. Lowering our catch into the boat, I said, "The water is like glass. Pull me back to the dock." John agreed.

It was a beautiful, clear afternoon. There were the usual thunder clouds building way out in the Atlantic, and a few over the mainland, but our air was as still and the water as flat as it ever got. I grabbed my ski and the rope and waded into the deeper water. Clyde and John pushed the boat off the bar. As soon as I was up, I began making some deep turns throwing up tall walls of clear water. I could hear them falling behind me. I wished there was a cute girl in the boat watching. If not Tracy, somebody.

As we approached the dock, I motioned for John to whip me into the shore. He nodded. Moments later he made his turn, and it was well timed. I easily coasted in, landing near the Jeep. I ran back to the boat to help them tie up and lift the trashcan of clams up to the dock.

Back at the house, we scrubbed and opened the clams. Sarah, meeting us with a large bowl, was quite pleased with their quality. Opening raw clams was the least fun part of the job, but repetition improved speed.

Taking the full bowl into the kitchen, we saw that the adults were brightly dressed and gathered around the bar talking, laughing, and pouring. Aunt Sarah thanked us and sent us to the showers to clean up for dinner.

In minutes, I was in a nice shirt and shorts. The fresh southwesterly breeze on the back steps quickly dried the remaining dampness from my skin. The pine hallway that ran through the house glowed with a golden light from the setting sun. The ladies enjoyed a lively conversation in the living room. The men were on the front deck, looking westward, across the sparkling ocean toward some towering thunderstorms off in the distance.

Charlie said, "Those storms are at least 40,000 feet tall, and fifty miles away, probably over Jacksonville."

"How can you tell? They look much closer," I said.

"In Navy navigational school, we learned how to judge the height, distance, and direction of thunderstorms. That squall line will not bother us tonight."

Bill Lawrence said, "Charlie, when did you start buying land out here?"

Puffing on his cigar, he said, "Well, a Canadian partner named Brian Newkirk and I started buying land in 1953 with the purpose of developing a unique beach resort. Five years later, O.T. Sloan joined me to buy Newkirk's 50% interest. Two years after that, Sam and Mary Carolyn bought O.T.'s interest and the development became a family project."

Dad jumped in to say, "When Mary Carolyn and I joined Charlie in '62, I oversaw the building of the A-Frame, or 'Charlie's Chapel' as we call it. To build up the dunes, for stabilizing the Cape and southern Core Banks, we bought a bulldozer. With the help of Tony Seaman, the Boy Scouts, and the Coast Guard, we planted 85,000 pine trees, many of which you see growing around us—"

"We helped too," I said.

"Yes. Sam, Clyde and John were a big help. I'd hoped to grow live oaks, but they don't grow well from seedlings in the salt spray. My plan was to plant pines on the ocean side and live oaks behind them. The pines would protect them initially from the salt spray. As the pines grew taller and were exposed to the more concentrated and constant salt spray, they would die, and allow the sufficiently mature live oaks to flourish.

"Unfortunately, the hybrid pines that Weyerhaeuser created for us were so good, they didn't die out. The live oaks were unable to survive in the shade."

Charlie said, "Sam's been a great and active partner, keeping us in good standing with the County agencies, the Army Corps of Engineers, and the local residents. He also did a great job building this house, didn't he?"

Everyone raised a glass in Dad's direction.

Nodding appreciatively, Dad said, "It was quite the feat building a structure like the A-Frame on this remote sandbar. The rafters consist of twenty-four fifty-foot pilings. That's a lot of heavy wood. Terry and I decided to drag them out here behind the Whirlwind. Unfortunately, a pop-up thunderstorm hit us in the middle of Back Sound. Waves broke some of the cables holding them together. It took us days to locate and gather the strays."

"Dad, the coals are ready," I announced at a pause in the conversation. The men followed him through the house toward the grill, stopping at the bar to freshen their cocktails.

Dad was a master steak griller and took great pains to ensure the meat was properly seasoned. According to him, seasoning was the foundation of a great steak, no matter how well it was cooked. He rarely delegated the critical role, but on this day, he had entrusted Isabel with the responsibility.

Isabel was busy in the kitchen, laughing and chatting with Sarah.

"Sam," she said, as he reached for the huge platter of beef, "Your steaks are ready and I'm pretty sure you'll like the results."

"You've never let me down, Iz."

The aromas wafting from the kitchen were almost too much anticipation for our quality-starved stomachs to bear. Isabel was one of the best cooks in town. Aunt Sarah excelled in seafood. Being in their favorite place in the world likely amplified the results. A feast was coming, and we could hardly wait.

The adults enjoyed their dinner at the kitchen counter, coffee table, and game table. We three ate on trays in the seating area. The meal was better than expected.

We called it a night about ten and the crowd continued late into the night.

twelve

Sailing with Mom

The following day, after breakfast, we split up to help our parents enjoy some activities. Clyde would take Aunt Sarah, Nan, Ellen, and Isabel to the beach. John would take Uncle Charlie, Dad, Bill, and Senator Staton offshore fishing. Mom said she wanted to go sailing. She and I would take the Sailfish in the shed that David had built from a kit, many years earlier.

The Sailfish was a blue flat-decked sailboat, thirteen feet long and four feet wide. It had a white triangular sail, speckled with some rust stains. The boat was like a Sunfish, without the cutout for your feet. Sailors stayed on it by standing on the downhill rail. It was little more than a shaped board with a sail.

John helped me carry it around front and Mom helped me rig it. When we were sure everything was secure, we pushed off into deeper water. We hopped aboard and sailed downwind, away from the beach.

I pushed the daggerboard down all the way when we were past the sandbars. A daggerboard is a four-foot piece of mahogany, about an inch thick and ten inches wide. It acts like a keel to keep the boat moving straight.

I steered for the mouth of the bight, trimming the sail as we turned toward the wind. The sleek boat lunged ahead with surprising speed and power.

Mom, seated forward of me, let go a "Weeee" as her hair tossed in the breeze.

We were heeled way over, standing on the downwind rail with our feet awash in the fast-moving water. Mom's fingers were tightly gripped on the mast.

"Mom, you doing OK?"

"Yes, honey, this is wonderful!"

We were making a good 15 miles-an-hour, given the size of the wake wave behind us.

"This is so much fun. This little boat is flying!"

In no time at all we passed through the bight and into the ocean. The swells were large. "Mom, we need to come about to get back into some calmer water. The boat'll slow down and flatten as I come into the wind to turn. When it does, duck and slide under the boom to the other side. Reposition, just like you are now. We need to do it quickly so we can keep the boat moving for control. Maybe we should have practiced this before we got in the ocean, but you're an old salt. You won't have any trouble."

"I appreciate your confidence," she said with a hint of hesitation.

"Don't worry, Mom, you'll do great."

I crested the next swell and surfed down its back into the trough, blocking some of the wind. In an easy voice, I said, "Ready about, hard-a-lee."

The little boat turned on a dime. As it flattened out, Mom and I both moved to the opposite side, just in time to surf the face of the swell that had come up behind us. I trimmed the sail and off we shot, back into the protected waters of the bight.

"Dad says there's thirty to forty feet of water below us right here. They call it Turtle Bay, I guess because of all the Loggerhead turtles that nest around here.

Following a couple of trips across the sound, I steered toward the marina and said, "Mom, what do you say we head over to Les and Sally's for a Coke?"

"That sounds like a wonderful idea. I'd love to see them."

Mom was fully relaxed now. Warmed by the morning sun, she soaked in the crystal-like water, the warm golden dunes and the waving green and sage sea oats. Puffy white clouds sailed majestically across a cerulean-blue sky.

"This is perfectly glorious," she said.

"Yes, it is. And it's great to be out here, with you."

We were skimming across the flat water, right on the edge of what that little boat could do. All of a sudden – Whack! We slammed to a stop. Mom went crashing into the mast and I into her as the bow dived under the water. Stunned, I slid back to the stern. "Mom, are you OK?"

"My shoulder hurts," rubbing it with a grimace. "I don't think it's serious though."

Looking around to see what we'd hit, there it was, just a couple of feet ahead of us. It was the biggest loggerhead turtle I'd ever seen. Her glassy eyes rolled slowly around in their sockets, dazed from the blow.

"Look mom!" pointing in her direction. "That's what we hit. Looks like we knocked her silly."

"Hello there old girl. We are so sorry."

"I don't think she can hear you over the ringing in her head right now."

Watching the turtle roll around in her daze, Mom rubbed her own shoulder and couldn't resist chuckling at the comedy of it all.

"How's your shoulder feel now?"

"It smarts, but I think it'll be alright."

"I'm glad, but it looks like it's starting to bruise. Let's get over to Sally's for some ice to put on it."

Before heading off, I pulled up the daggerboard to check it for damage. It had a one-inch dent about eight inches long on its leading edge. I reinserted it as the turtle rolled over and submerged, not to be seen again.

"That had to hurt. I hope she'll be OK," Mom said sweetly.

"Well, they're probably called Loggerheads for good reason. I'm sure she'll be OK.

We took our positions, trimmed the sail in, and resumed our track toward the marina, more slowly than before. I sailed straight to the shore and beached the boat left of the dock. The tide was falling, so it wasn't necessary to pull her very high on the beach.

"You go on ahead Mom. I'll get the sail down and follow shortly."

Sally Moore was a no-nonsense lady who ran a tight ship. She had a tanned leather-like face, deeply etched by the island's elements. Her golden hair framed gleaming blue eyes, and a joyful smile gave her a rustic beauty all her own. She had a deep respect for and devotion to this, her island paradise. She embodied the Cape for all who knew her. If *National Geographic* ever did a feature on Cape Lookout, Sally's face would be the cover.

She was barely taller than the broom she kept close by, in her never-ending struggle against sand that found its way into her shop by wind and untrained customers – a mistake she allowed only once. Her regulars knew that clean feet were her price of admission.

"Well, hello, Mary." Sally gleamed. "It's good to see you. How've you been sweetie?" Her unfiltered Camel cigarette bounced up and down like a director's baton metering every syllable of her Down East brogue.

"Hello Sally. I'm well, thank you. I hope the boys haven't given you any trouble."

"Not as far as we know, but there's still plenty of summer left."

"Ha, Miss Sally, would you mind making an ice bag for Mom's shoulder?" I asked. "We ran into a turtle out there and Mom banged her shoulder against the mast pretty hard."

"Oh no, I'm sorry to hear that. Let's get you fixed up, darlin'." Sally went to work putting some ice into a clean washcloth.

"You sit down over here and hold this on your shoulder. Now, what can I get you?"

Mom ordered a Coke and started her story about our turtle encounter. As she recounted the adventure, I got up to look at Sally's shell and bottle collections. There were lots of new ones since last year. It had been a light season for hurricanes, so I guessed the winter's steady parade of nor'easters had raked them ashore.

The front of the store was filled with shelves and wall hooks around the windows. They held all kinds of fishing tackle, Clarke Spoons, dried foods, mosquito repellants, sunscreens, peanut butter, and sardines – everything the weekend fisherman needed for a day or night on the water.

Underneath the windows were coolers, filled with bait, soft drinks, and beer. Even ice, the most precious commodity on Cape Lookout, was available, but at a price that reflected the cost of the gasoline and propane to store it.

The wall at the end of the counter was shelved floor-to-ceiling with Sally's shell and bottle collections. As a resident on the island, she was first out after the storms to find bottles and shells of a variety and quality that mainland collectors rarely encountered.

She had the largest collection of Scotch Bonnets I'd ever seen. The Bonnet is North Carolina's state seashell, but knew of no one, other than Sally, who'd found a whole one. And she had dozens.

"Mom, look at all these Scotch Bonnets," I interrupted.

"My goodness," Mom said. "I've only found a few broken ones. Yours are beautiful."

Sally grinned proudly and said, "They appear on the beaches after those hurrycanes. There's usually a few of them on the east beach after a good nor'easter."

Sally's bottle collection was legend. She had all sizes, shapes, and colors, squeezed into the space available. The prettiest ones were rich violet and emerald. Many had raised or etched lettering to identify their contents of medicines, oils, spices, wine, rum, and spirits with dates as far back as the late 1500's.

As I carefully lifted one, Sally said, "That one contained poison. See those Xs etched into the neck? They were added warning to the holder that its contents were lethal.

Each bottle was a window into the lives of the sea voyagers who had held them hundreds of years ago as they explored and supplied the New World from England, Portugal, and Spain. Their pristine beauty was ironic, given the horrible fate their owners had suffered in the treacherous waters that surrounded us. When held, they seemed to emit a mysterious, electrical-like connection to the person who'd held it hundreds of years before. I shivered at the reminder that more than 5,000 seagoing communities had met their violent demise, so close by.

Mom was winding up her conversation with Sally when she turned to me to say, "Son, we'd better get back to the house. I promised Nan and Iz that I'd walk with them after lunch."

Sally said, "I hope your shoulder feels better soon honey."

"Thank you, Sally," Mom responded, "I'll bring Nan and Iz by later this afternoon. They will want to see you and how much your collection has grown."

I sailed as straight a path as possible through the shallow water to get mom back to the house. I could tell she was hurting, but she rarely complained. It was not her nature to discuss her pains.

"Mom, I met a girl earlier this summer. I felt she was someone I could happily spend the rest of my life with. She liked me a lot too, but she had a boyfriend. I don't think I'll ever find another like her."

"Oh son, I'm sorry, I know that hurts, but don't despair. The perfect girl is out there, just waiting to be swept off her feet by you. You'll find her. I have no doubt."

"Thanks Mom. I've really enjoyed our time this morning. I know sailing's not your favorite thing to do, and you got hurt doing it today."

"It's not so much the activity that matters to me. It's being with you, our family, and our friends that I adore. I can handle some discomforts to be with the people I love."

"I love you, Mom," I said as I thought about how hard she worked in the background to entertain and clean to make sure everyone enjoyed themselves. I often wished she would relax some of her concerns to be *with* us more.

"Well, I'm really glad you wanted to come sailing with me today. I'm sorry about your shoulder. How's it feeling?"

True to character, she said, "The ice helped. It doesn't even bother me now."

As we approached the beach in front of the A-Frame, Sarah, Isabel, and Nan were sunning in beach chairs on the side deck. Izzy got up to wave hello, leaned over the deck rail, and asked how our sail was.

"Lots to tell," Mom said. I'll be up in a jiff, and we'll catch up."

I watched her join them as I dragged the boat ashore and stowed the mast and sail. They hovered around her like nurses. They examined her shoulder, then made her comfortable in a nearby chair. Nan appeared with a compress of some sort.

thirteen

The Parents' Last Night

When I entered the shed, Clyde's legs protruded from under the Jeep. "What are you doing?" I asked.

"There's too much play in the steering linkage."

"OK, when you finish, I could use a hand storing the Sailfish."

"Won't be much longer. Putting the cover on now."

The flatbed roared up the back drive with the fishermen all smiles. With the motor stopped, Bill and Charlie were arguing over who caught the largest sea bass. Charlie claimed weight and Bill, length.

Charlie called over to me, "Sam are there any scales in there or in the kitchen?"

"No sir, no scales that I know of."

"Well," Bill said, "guess I'm the winner. Mine's clearly longer than yours."

Charlie laughed and said, "OK, I concede."

Sarah opened the cooler and said "Golly Miss Sally, look at these beautiful fish. We'll have a seafood bash tonight."

We began unloading the flatbed when, as expected, Aunt Sarah said, "Boys we'll need some fresh clams this afternoon. Oh, and while you're out, pick up ten pounds of shrimp at Harkers from Mr. Credle."

"Yes ma'am," Clyde replied, "We'll get them after lunch."

"Brown noser," John cracked as he lifted the cooler off the bed. After cleaning the fish, we headed inside for some hot vegetable soup and grilled cheese sandwiches. The beachcombers showed off their shells. Bill told an animated story of the one that got away. Mom captured the room when she recounted our adventure with the sea turtle.

After lunch, we collected our clamming gear and cooler, for the shrimp, and headed for the boat. We'd decided to try the spot where we were so lucky before. In no time at all, we'd filled our bucket and were off to Harkers.

The marina was busy with Saturday boaters heading out for the day and fishermen returning with their catches. The office was filled with weekend motel guests getting ice cream and boaters buying last minute supplies.

"Hello Mr. Credle. How are things?" John asked as he placed the cooler on the counter. "Can we get ten pounds of shrimp, please sir?"

"How're you boys doing? Are your parents enjoying themselves?" He placed the cooler on the scale and started filling it.

"They're having a great time," I answered. "They send their best and hope to see you soon. Dad said he plans to be back in a couple of weeks to meet with some of the locals about the Park Service. He'll be staying here at the motel."

"I look forward to it. Please tell all of them I said hello."

"Yessir, we will," John said.

Clyde called skiing on the way back to the Cape. He used the sticks of the S-turns like a slalom course, pulling some sand up on their shallow sides.

When we got back to the house, we quickly cleaned and opened the clams, headed and shelled the shrimp. We used the rest of the afternoon to grade the driveway and replace the bent Marston mats.

"Looks like 'ole Uncle Charlie knows what he's talking about," Clyde said. "This driveway's like a tennis court now."

Our seafood dinner was another feast. We ate it more slowly than usual, enjoying what would be our last gourmet meal for a long time. When the adults finished, we cleared and washed dishes to let them enjoy the evening. I dried and stacked plates at the counter, so I could better hear the men's conversation in the living room.

Charlie said in raised voice, "Congress passed the bill for the Cape Lookout National Seashore and Johnson signed it three years ago. Since then, the state has never reached out to us or to the Core Banks Rod and Gun Club. You'd think they'd at least check in with the two largest tract owners."

"The Carteret planning board has stone-walled us at every turn," Dad said. "They listen to our requests, throw up arguments they can't substantiate, and respond 'Too bad,' when we talk about our rights as property owners."

"Looks like they've closed the door on offers and development," Senator Staton said. "Condemnation proceedings will likely start soon. The sole issue will be price."

"Well, you're sitting on paradise here and I know you want to enjoy it as long as you can," Isabel said.

"Paradise until the bugs find you," Mom said. "This house, with its screens and conveniences, is what makes it paradise out here,"

The pain in her shoulder had likely dissolved her ability to hold back her disgust for the biting monsters. She was right. The A-Frame made life at the Cape enjoyable, offering time for reflection rather than survival.

Paul spoke up in Mom's defense. "Seems to me that some sort of public facilities out here would allow folks with similar objections to Mary Carolyn's, a more civilized way to spend some time out here."

"Well," Isabel said, "I'm going out to brave the mosquitoes and enjoy those amazing stars."

"That's a great idea," Bill said as Paul, Dad, and others followed her through the front door.

The heavens were putting on a show. The group was immediately spellbound. I slipped back into the house and turned off the lights that weren't needed by those who remained inside. I grabbed a couple cans of mosquito repellant from the cabinet on the way out the back door.

The group was in silent reverence. There were occasional observations of the amazing colors in the Milky Way and the difficulty of distinguishing constellations in the bright stardust of thousands of smaller, yet brilliantly distinct stars. Each pinpoint of light pierced minute patches of coal-black darkness. Stars were layered upon each other, giving the distinct impression of depth.

"I feel like I'm floating in space," Izzy said.

"They're so close, I could just pluck one from the sky," Mom agreed.

Paul said, There's Orion."

Bill followed, "There's the Big Dipper and the Small Dipper."

They stood there, in childlike wonder and awe of God's amazing creation.

"It is a shame more people can't experience this," Isabel said to everyone's agreement.

Dad emerged from the front door with his banjo, took a seat at the corner of the front deck. He began quietly strumming. I handed off the two mosquito spray cans and left the group to enjoy their last night in paradise.

The next morning was abuzz with packing, organizing and promises to return soon. Breakfast with eggs, bacon and pancakes was on the counter for pick-up as they worked. This crowd was as energetic in their exits as they were in their arrivals.

Over the clamor, Charlie called out, "John, let's get these bags loaded. We'll be ready to head for the plane soon," which meant, he was ready to go and anyone who wanted to fly with him had better snap-to as well.

Clyde and I helped John load the bags onto the flatbed, which sat atop the newly renovated steel-matted driveway. Clyde and I would stay to help the sailboat crew get ready to embark.

As we tied down the last of the bags, Charlie and Sarah came down the back stairs with the Statons. Aunt Sarah gave us a hug and thanked us for our care and attention. The Statons added their thanks, and Charlie, not to be left out, said, "Good job on the driveway boys. The Seabees couldn't have done a better job."

"Thank you, Uncle Charlie," we said, looking at each other with a mix of pride and surprise at his glowing compliment.

With all aboard, John backed down the drive and roared off toward the airstrip. Watching them ride away, I thought, how remarkable it was to have a dream and turn it into reality. Thanks to Uncle Charlie's vision, many now enjoy this amazing place.

As the roar of the flatbed faded, I turned back toward the A-Frame to hear the happy clamor of the *Quintet* crew inside, readying for their sail home. The two crowds were so different. Uncle Charlie and Dad were oil and water, but I loved and respected them both. I aspired to emulate the best qualities of each of them. Charlie shaped his world, with logic, urging and grit. Dad reflected the world he encountered, with art, music, and word. Charlie travelled fast and Dad slow, but they both got where they were going.

When they worked together, they accomplished much. I stood on the deck of a beautiful, sturdy A-Frame house, built on shifting sand. It had been enjoyed by countless families and groups through the years. It all began ten years earlier, with lines drawn on a napkin, as the two of them enjoyed lunch.

Back in the kitchen, Isabel, Mom, and Nan packed the travel coolers and discussed leftovers and how to leave it for us. Dad, Bill, and Paul stood in the living room discussing the trip back.

Clyde and I carried the bags to the back porch for John's return in the flatbed. When we finished, we sat at the counter and enjoyed the remaining pancakes, bacon, biscuits, and juice. Dad's biscuits rivaled Walter's and his pancakes were the clear winner, though we never shared that with Walter.

When I heard the flatbed coming, I let Dad know.

"We're ready when he gets here," Dad said.

"But we sure hate to leave," Izzy added, forcing a sad tone through a demeanor that found delight in everything.

"You boys have been wonderful hosts, we can't thank you enough," Mom said.

"How's your shoulder feel today?" I asked.

Raising her sleeve to reveal a large bruise, Mom said, "It looks a lot worse than it hurts."

"I'm sorry Mom. I hope you will sail with me again."

"I will sail with you any time, dear boy."

I hugged her, avoiding her shoulder, and she squeezed back with her good arm. Clyde, Bill, and I picked up the coolers from the kitchen on our way out. John had parked the flatbed beside the Jeep for easy loading. We were off quickly.

The trip to the boat was more subdued than the arrival had been, but everyone was upbeat. Their sail back to Morehead would take three hours and their ride back to Sanford, about the same. They were most likely conserving energy for the journey.

Getting gear and people aboard the boat was fast. They worked efficiently to stow luggage, coolers, and ready the sails. Dad started the engine, looked around, and gave the order to cast off lines.

As he backed the *Quintet* out of the basin, dock lines were coiled and stowed. After cruising a short distance into the channel, Dad brought her into the wind and within moments, all three sails rose gracefully up the masts. They luffed and cracked loudly in the stiffening breeze until they snapped taught when he bore off the wind and headed toward the ocean.

The crowd waved and shouted goodbyes. The rapidly expanding gulf of water between us made me feel something like homesickness. It had been a special time with our parents that I was sure I'd remember always.

fourteen

On the Moon, Just Like Neil Armstrong

In the days following our parents' visit, Clyde and John had decided to stay on the Cape rather than return to Sanford with me to watch the Apollo 11 moon mission from takeoff to splashdown. They planned to follow it on the radio and watch the moon walk at the marina.

From the age of 10, I had been a huge nerd for America's space program. For each Gemini and Apollo mission, I was glued to the TV. If spacewalks or dockings were scheduled on a school day, you could bet I'd have a thermometer resting on my bedroom radiator, heating to a temperature that would qualify me for a sick day at home.

Driving home in my Mustang the haunting, lonesome lyrics of David Bowie's "Space Oddity" reminded me of the pain I'd had in high school. Had my circuit gone dead? What happened to my confidence? How had I become so shy and withdrawn – alone in space?

I grew up with the kids that had become the 'in-crowd,' but I was no longer *in*, rather I was made to feel out. When I approached, they were hurtful or cleverly insulting. Here I was, all alone, floating in my tin can.

High school had been a cruel playground and I often felt like the last one picked. I didn't make the football team, was unwelcome in the cool section at the Dairy Bar, and suffered countless crash-and-burns when I asked A-list girls on dates.

One of the reasons I liked the space program so much was that those guys were pros at managing setbacks. They continually pushed the edge of the envelope and learned from their failures until they got it right. Once they got it right, they went on to do great things, like putting a man on the moon.

I got it right with Tracy when I stepped over the edge, outside of my tin can, to experience the strange and dangerous world of love. It didn't work out, but what a success it was for me – a successful failure. Tracy showed me what was possible beyond the edge of my setbacks – really great things.

The next four days were spent in front of our TV in our den, watching every moment of coverage. I missed only a few commercials for bathroom and food breaks. When Neil Armstrong's foot stepped onto the surface of the moon, my hopes soared. I was right there with him. "That's one small step for man, one giant leap for mankind."

When Armstrong and Aldren took off from the lunar surface in the lunar excursion module to join Michael Collins in the command capsule and head home, I decided to do the same. It had been a nice visit in Sanford, with Mom, Dad, my sister Emily, and the men aboard Apollo 11, but it was time to get back to the Cape.

The vastness of space and the desolation of the Moon fascinated me. But Cape Lookout was accessible. Time spent there transformed my emptiness of loneliness into the fullness of solitude. In the transcendental vacuum of the Cape, away from the world's noise, confusion, and hurt, I could hear the comforting voice of God.

Photos

A-Frame Aerial

A-Frame Side

A-Frame Front

Interior Kitchen

Interior Seating and Bar

Porthole

Coast Guard Station and Maritime Forest

Uncle Charlie Landing

Dad - Sam Bass Sr. instructs Boy Scouts, Sam, and Clyde on tree planting.

fifteen

Henry

On a trip to Harkers Island for groceries, we heard that our friend Henry Long had landed on the island a couple of days earlier. We decided to visit him when we got back to the Cape.

"Can't believe we didn't see him come in," John said.

"Yeah, we've been busy fixing the Jeep's axle. Guess we just didn't look over at the right times," Clyde said. "It's riding pretty well, if I do say so myself."

"We helped a little too, you know?" I added.

As we pulled into the Long's drive, Henry popped out of the back screen door and waved with a smile.

"Hey man," John called out.

"How're you guys doing? Sam, Clyde, it's been a while. John, it's great to be away from VES, huh?"

"Great summer so far. Heard you got down a couple of days ago. You should have come over," John said.

"Yeah, haven't felt much like socializing. Just been hanging out here and surfing some. But it's good to see you guys. I was getting a little bored."

"Why don't you stay with us?" John said. "No sense being over here all alone."

"OK. It'd be kinda nice hanging out with you boys at the Frame. Give me a minute to throw some stuff in a bag."

Henry disappeared for a couple minutes then emerged with his duffle saying, "I'll need to empty the fridge, shut off the gas, and close up the cottage."

"We can help with that," John said.

Each of us took a job to make quick work of closing up. Henry's bag, food, ski and surfboard loaded on the flatbed, we headed back to the A-Frame, with little idea of how much more firepower we'd just added to our adventures.

Henry seemed even more melancholy, having taken off for a walk along the sound toward the lighthouse. Clyde and John tinkered in the shed with the Jeep's transfer case. I flipped through a thick book titled, "The Graveyard of the Atlantic" and the radio played in the background.

After dinner we played some cards, listened to tunes, and called it a night, earlier than usual. There was a little extra conversation before nodding off with Henry in the room, but sleep came soon.

Morning sunlight beamed into the bedroom and a fresh breeze puffed through the screens. Looking forward to adding Henry's energy to our adventures, I reached for the radio and cranked it wide open and was delighted to hear The Crazy World of Arthur Brown screaming "Fire." It was time to burn.

A colorful new batch of obscenities filled the room, with Henry's addition to the band. I pulled on my shorts and walked down the back stairs to the deck to begin the new day.

After cereal, we loaded gear, drinks, and a fresh tank of gas into the boat for a day's skiing. The sky was mostly clear with moderate winds from the southwest. Skiing would be good along the western shores of Core Banks.

John slowed to a stop at the beginning of the course. Clyde tossed out a ski rope and Henry rolled over the side, ski in hand. Before the line was tight, he yelled, "Hit it."

With a jerk, he was up and making deep cuts and sharp turns that produced giant walls of water. His wake jumps landed him well beyond the opposite wake. Occasionally he'd grab his ski and tuck it under him to fly far above the water clearing it by at least four feet. Henry was an amazing skier.

After a couple of rounds of skiing for each of us, Clyde said, "Hey, John, will you pull the three of us?"

"Sure," he said. "There's a good place up ahead to drop." Pulling multiple skiers requires each skier to get up fast on two skis creating as little drag as possible on the old motor. We dropped the extra skis where we could collect them later.

Clyde tossed three lines over the stern one-by-one, to avoid tangling. We all jumped in and were ready fast. When the longest rope handle reached me, I gave John the signal.

We all popped up quickly, but no one took a breath until we emerged from the thick cloud of blue smoke billowing from the old engine under strain. At John's signal, we dropped our extra skis, and he pulled us back out to the channel.

The water was calm, and the boat was fast. Clyde, on the middle rope cut toward me with his butt skimming the water as low as he could get and shot under my rope. He immediately cut back hard to avoid running into Henry and crossed back under my rope again.

I gave him a thumbs up and yelled, "Let me know next time and I'll make it harder for you."

Henry yelled to get our attention. He signaled for us to pull into the wake behind the boat. Nodding, Clyde, and I swung in, with Clyde just ahead of me.

Henry held his rope handle chest level indicating the height he wanted our ropes for his coming trick. Clyde and I looked at each other, amazed.

"Are you crazy?" Clyde yelled to Henry.

He laughed wildly, and screamed, "You know it man!"

His face now serious, he turned hard away from us. As far out as he could get, he cut back our way, slingshotting toward us at maximum speed. The turn left a huge rooster tail and pulled the boat toward him. His eyes focused intently on the wake as he approached it and us. With perfect timing, he uncoiled like a spring right atop the wave and launched skyward. As he rose, he grabbed his ski and tucked it under him to fly over our ski ropes, with more than a foot to spare.

His landing was just as spectacular, absorbing the five-foot fall and cutting back to join us in the wake. As we cheered his jump, Clyde and I looked at each other in agreement. We were outclassed.

But undaunted, I threw my rope over Clyde and cut hard to take my turn. With all my weight on the tail of my ski, I began a series of deep, smooth cuts producing long, tall, rows of sparkling water, one after another. They hung in the air like wrinkled crystal.

When I took a breather, Henry and Clyde resumed ducking and jumping each other's ropes, gradually increasing the difficulty. We were having a great time one-upping each other.

Apparently reaching the limit of his ability while jumping over Henry's rope, Clyde caught the tip of his ski and collided with Henry on the way down. Together, they hit the water in a ball of arms, legs, skis, and heads rolling through and over the water. I turned toward them and released to help if needed.

Clyde popped up first, and spewed about a gallon of seawater while signaling he was OK. Henry followed with a full-throated laugh and fist pump. Seeing that they had survived the collision, John took off to collect the dropped skis before returning to pick us up.

As we climbed into the boat, Clyde laughed and said, "Man, that was awesome. Great job tossing your rope Henry, so it wouldn't snap my neck."

Noticing a cut on Henry's chin, I said, "Looks like you got the short end. What happened?"

Unfazed, Henry replied, "I'm not sure whether it was Clyde, his ski, or my ski handle, but it was really cool watching all those stars as we rolled through the water."

"That's got to hurt," I said.

"Not so much," Henry replied, "but let's get over to Sally's for some ice and lunch. I'm hungry."

We all agreed and headed for the marina. Nearing the pier, we saw Les cranking up a 55-gallon drum of gasoline from his boat with the davit, mounted to the dock. We tied up well away from the fueling area as it was one of Les's strictest rules to keep it clear.

Les' dock was very high, like the Coast Guard dock was. There was a six-foot climb up the ladder from our boat at low tide. Reaching the top was no reward. The splintery deck boards were skillet-hot in the noon sun, so we didn't stand around.

We sprinted down to the end and asked if he needed any help. We stood in a tight group in the shadow that was created by the small pile of supplies he had stacked on the dock. Les transported all of the marina's inventory by himself. He was tall and lean with arms the size of our thighs. He looked like the sailor on one of those WWII posters in a tight rolled-up shirt that was about to split under the pressure of his bulging biceps. He was soft spoken, unless we crossed a line we shouldn't. When that happened, he was as tough as our dads, and he was never shy of filling the role when required.

He was always willing to teach when we had a problem. Rather than just give us a quick answer, he provided several solutions for tackling issues that came up regularly on the Cape. We learned because he took the time to show us how, rather than just fixing it.

"Hello boys, you having a play day?"

"Yessir." Clyde answered. "Our parents kept us pretty busy last week, so we needed a break," he said. Can we help you?"

"No, this is the last of it for now," Les said. "You going in for some lunch?"

"Yes sir, and some ice for Henry's face," John said.

"Yeah, I just noticed that, Henry," Les said. "How did the other fellow come out?"

Looking at Clyde, Henry said, "As far as I can tell, unscratched. We had a small collision out there. Guess I ran into his ski."

"Well, you boys do play rough. Try not to kill each other. Your parents would have my hide if I let that happen. Go on in now and let Sally have a look."

"Yessir." We took off in a sprint down the long, piping-hot deck. My mouth began to water as I anticipated one of her delicious Stewart sandwiches with an ice-cold Orange Crush or Grape NEHI. Lunch at Miss Sally's was one of the best treats on the Cape.

As we took our seats at the counter, she said, "What'll it be gentlemen?"

John ordered a Coke with a ham and cheese sandwich. We followed in turn. Sally popped the bottle tops off with quick yanks and slid each bottle down the counter to us. She pulled four cellophane-wrapped sandwiches from the cooler and placed two of them in the Stewart infrared oven, closed the door, and gave the dial a quick spin.

Henry then asked, "Sally, could I get a piece of ice for my chin?"

"Let me take a look at that. Hmm, that needs a stitch, but I've got a butterfly bandage that'll do the trick." Reaching under the counter, she pulled out a large first aid kit that looked more professional than the little box we had at the house. She cleaned the wound and handed Henry a piece of ice wrapped in a clean dish cloth.

Sally pulled the heated sandwiches from the oven, removed their plastic bags, and served them to us.

"Henry?" Sally asked, "what's going on at your house?" The Long cottage was in clear sight of Sally and Les' place, about a quarter of a mile away.

Henry answered, "It was just me there for a few days until I moved to the Frame with the boys. This weekend my mom and aunt are coming with four girl cousins. I'll stay with these guys as long as they'll have me.

Sally nodded with a smile.

"How's your dad?" she asked.

"He's doing well. He's supposed to fly in when mom comes down."

Les walked in just in time to hear and said, "My runway's a mess. I'll stop by the A-Frame tomorrow, pick up the bulldozer and smooth it out before he needs it."

"Thank you, Mr. Moore, he really appreciates that," Henry responded. "I appreciate it even more. A couple of years ago, he had to land on the beach when the field was full of water. He set down successfully, from what I could see from the car. When he taxied over the tidal berm, the tail shot up in a huge cloud of sand and a terrible roar. It scared me to death.

"When I got to the plane, Daddy was OK, and he'd pulled the tail down. He greeted me with a box of groceries saying he needed to get back to Beaufort to check the plane out before the mechanics left for the weekend.

He said, 'Son, I'm going to need you to hold the tail down until I can get enough pull from the prop to get the plane back onto the beach for takeoff.'"

"How long do I hang on Daddy?"

"As long as you can, son."

"I learned what leading edges were that day." He pointed to his nose, forehead, and shins. "I had shorts and a tee shirt on, like we do pretty much all the time out here. When Daddy throttled up, the prop blasted me with sand and shells that gnawed the skin off my leading edges.

"I held on to keep from falling as the plane began to move faster than I could keep up. Daddy finally stuck his arm out the window to tell me to let go. When I did, I tumbled head over heels for a dozen yards or so until rolling to a painful stop."

Pointing to divots and scars on his legs, Henry said, "When I showed these to Daddy, know what he said? 'Next time Son, wear long sleeves and pants.' Daddy never asked us to do anything he thought was too hard, but he sure had a mighty high opinion of our abilities."

"Boys, your dads served well in a war that was tough on them. I suspect it's why they raise you with such high expectations." Sally tossed John and Clyde's empty paper plates into the trash as she continued. "You know Les, served in the Army and fought at Okinawa and Guadalcanal before being stationed here. He was involved in a raid that captured several American traitors and U-Boat sailors just north of here," pointing toward the lighthouse as she continued. "There were a few Harkers Islanders who were supplying U-Boat crews with food and water at drop spots along Core Banks."

"Wow," I said. "I never heard that story. Guess that's how Les wound up here from Indiana, huh?"

"That's right," Sally said. "I met him just after he was re-stationed here. We dated for four months and were married in a chapel on the base."

I took another bite of my hamburger, and marveled that it was heated all the way through without melting the cellophane. "Sally," I asked, "how does that oven work?"

"I wish I could tell you darlin'. All I know is it's infra-red or something like that."

"Hmm, sure does make a sandwich taste good."

"As good as these things can taste anyway." Sally added.

"Wind's out of the east," Henry said. "Let's ski over at Barden's inlet. I think the water'll be flat there, close in on the lee shore.

"Be careful of the shoaling over there," Sally said as she reached for our lunch ticket. "One of you please sign this for your account."

Clyde took it and said, "Thank you Sally. This was the best lunch we've had since our folks left." Sally smiled as she said, "You boys don't starve over there. Come on back any time, and I'll feed you."

"Yes ma'am. We will for sure," Clyde said.

The weathered gray boards of Les's dock had only gotten hotter during our lunch. We ran hard for the ladder, hopping and screaming to rush those ahead of us. Unwilling to fry our feet any further, Henry and I jumped in, near the boat.

As we motored our way over to Barden's Inlet, Henry asked John, "Do you think this motor's got enough power to pull me barefoot? The water's perfect for it."

"It takes her a while to plane, but I think it'll work if you drop a ski."

"Sounds good," Henry said, and he was over the side and up on his slalom in a snap. When the Whirlwind was up to full speed, Henry planted his left foot in the water and created a spray that enveloped him. Soon after, his ski popped up behind him, and he was bare-footing.

It took every bit of strength he had to stay up as he dragged deep in the water. He fought it for a while, then tried a spin, only to go tumbling.

When we circled back, Clyde, said, "Let me show you guys the skivvy-blow-out. John, get me on a run, wide open with plenty of water ahead. When I signal, cut the wheel as hard to the right as you can without flipping."

With Clyde up and the boat going full speed, he shot across the wake toward the right side and gave the signal. As John started his turn hard to the right, Clyde turned sharply to sling shot back across the wake and out as far to the left as he could go. Leaning out as hard as he could, he was skimming across the water at least twice our speed, putting him at more than sixty miles-per-hour. When he could go no faster, he jumped out of his ski and landed butt-first to slide for yards and yards, before tumbling to splashy and wild applause.

"So, what about your skivvies?" Henry asked.

"That one didn't do it, but these cutoffs are tough. Surf baggies are a different story . . . they blow out easily."

We each took turns trying the blowout and agreed it was a permanent addition to our catalogue.

As the afternoon wore on, we tried many new stunts including flips and gainers off the top of the motor, sometimes stopped, sometimes with a skier. Each new antic stoked another, 'Hey y'all, watch this.'

The *Diamond City* ferry had gone by several times during the day, without any mention. But, on her last trip of the day—when she was heavily laden with tired, sunburnt tourists—Henry got that crazy look in his eyes.

"Pull alongside her and match speed as close as you can and still keep me up."

"OK," John said as Clyde, and I grinned at each other.

Moments later, Henry was up, and we were heading for the *Diamond City*.

John approached the ferry from her stern and pulled along her port side. He left enough room between us for Henry to maneuver. We were glad to see our friend Bud Doughton at the helm with no sign of Captain Josiah Bailey.

Henry ran his hand gracefully along the top rail as he skied alongside the boat. He seemed to be having a conversation with a couple of cute girls he passed. Bud smiled and pointed down.

"I think he's saying that Captain Bailey's down below," I yelled."

By now, Henry was signaling for another pass. The look on his face suggested something different. When I gestured a guess of his intentions, he grinned and gave me an enthusiastic thumb's-up.

I went forward to relay the plan. John smiled and began his second approach, this time in a wider faster circle, accelerating to full speed as we approached the ferry.

Above the engine's roar came a booming voice on the *Diamond City's* loudspeaker. "Boys, don't come any closer to this vessel."

"Oh crap, that's Cap'n Bailey." John screamed. But the revelation had no apparent impact on his or Henry's resolve as we continued speeding toward the ferry. John timed his turn perfectly, swinging Henry toward the middle of the sailboat for a long, sweeping arc that laid a beautiful sheet of refreshing sea water over every weary soul aboard.

Screams of surprise, delight, and anger were heard above the roar of our outboard. Looking over his shoulder, Henry gave a mock tip of his hat as we sped away and emptied our lungs with laughter.

We dragged Henry aboard and headed back to the A-Frame, reveling in success. Henry and John started their showers, and I got the grill fired up and pulled out some hamburger patties from the freezer.

The A-Frame's front windows were filled with the brilliant colors of sunset. Stevie Wonder's "My Cherie Amour," reminded me of Tracy. *How I had wished that she was mine.* I grabbed the radio and walked to the front porch to watch the sunset. As the sky darkened, lightning illuminated distant clouds with large puffs of yellow and white. The Classics IV sang "Traces," and I thought—that's all there will ever be of Tracy—and even those were fading.

John came from the bathroom and yelled, "Next."

"John, the burgers are mostly thawed. If you'll get 'em started, I'll take over after my shower."

"Yeah, sure," he answered.

As I passed Clyde at the kitchen counter, I said, "Looks like thunderstorms tonight. We'd better close up down here when we head up for bed."

After supper we listened to tunes and played some cards. Thunderstorms pounded through the night, all around us. We were quickly awakened when one deluged our beds. After furiously closing the bedroom portholes, we rushed downstairs to seal up the first floor, having forgotten to do so earlier. The rest of the evening was a damp, muggy mess.

Next morning, after breakfast, we took off to do some more skiing. Henry was on the line when we spotted Mason Williams entering the bight on his 28'

Bertram, the *Harkaway*. It looked like Travis was with him on the flying bridge. Henry saw them moments later and motioned to circle around behind him so he could come alongside for another ski-by. John gave a thumbs up and headed for Mason, who was now in the middle of the bight. As we passed them, we waved and saw their surfboards sticking out of the cockpit.

John made a tight turn around and brought Henry alongside. As we passed by, John slowed to a speed just a little faster than the Bertram. Henry could have jumped in as he ran his hand along the entire length of the boat, chatting with Travis.

He followed the curve around toward the bow of the boat. For reasons that remain a mystery, Henry's ski rope went slack, and he went down. He suddenly vanished under the bow of that 28-foot Bertram churning through the water at twenty-five miles-per-hour. Mason immediately pulled back on his throttles, but not in time. John spun around and pulled up beside the stopped Bertram. Travis and Mason were frantically looking all around the boat for any sign of Henry, focusing mostly on the patch of splintered ski remains.

"Oh no, we've killed Henry!" Clyde moaned.

Before any of us dived in to look for him – up he pops – between the two boats shouting, "Fooled ya."

"You crazy idiot!" Mason shouted, "We thought you were dead."

"You'd better stay clear of *me*. I'll kill you," Travis shouted.

Henry laughed so hard I don't think he heard any of our rants. He said only, "What a trip man. That was awesome."

"How did you miss those propellors?" Mason asked.

After catching his breath, Henry answered, "When I felt my ski on the bottom of the boat, I pushed away as hard as I could. My feet popped out when I swam down. I looked up just in time to see the props grind my ski to smithereens. That's when it occurred to me to hang out on the bottom for a little fun."

"You demented wacko," Travis shouted as Mason stopped him from diving on top of Henry.

Shaking it off, Travis said, "Well, we came out here to surf. If we can't kill Henry, let's go ride a few."

Dragging Henry onboard, we followed the *Harkaway* to the dock. After a quick stop at the A-Frame for our boards, we were off to the beach.

The waves were good. Travis and Mason had an uncanny knack for showing up when surf conditions were excellent. Today was no exception. As soon as the truck rolled to a stop, we all headed into the breakers. Any remaining conflict between Travis and Henry was washed away in the suds.

The hours passed quickly. Around four-thirty Mason called over to Travis and said, "We'd better be getting back."

"Why don't you guys stay the night?" I asked.

"Wish we could, but Travo and I've got a function tonight. We're already late."

We drove them back to the dock as fast as the Jeep would carry us. Moments later, they were aboard the *Harkaway* catching the dock lines we tossed them. With a roar of the engines and white water spraying behind, they raced off into the setting sun.

We motored back to the A-Frame. Clyde and John headed for the showers. Henry and I grabbed colas from the fridge and took a couple of chairs onto the front deck to watch the sun go down.

For a while, we just sat, staring at the blazing clouds and sun near the golden ocean.

Then, I blurted out, "Henry, why do you do everything on the edge?" Seems like you don't care – almost like you're *trying* to kill yourself."

After a pause he began, "As a kid, my dad and uncle told wild stories about their adventures growing up. It seemed like they were saying they didn't want us boys to grow up like namby-pambies. I *wanted* to be just like my daddy was.

I pushed every sport and activity, like you say, right to the edge. Things are just more exciting that way.

"I don't know, I've bounced back from some pretty serious crashes. I guess I've become comfortable with risk. Might even need it. I wouldn't actually *try* to kill myself, but if a Bertram or a ferry did kill me, guess that'd be OK."

"Wow, man. That's intense . . . But I don't believe it. I think you enjoy dancing on the edge way too much to give it up. You said this afternoon you pushed off that Bertram's bottom with everything you had, to clear those propellers.

"No, buddy, in that split second, I believe you wanted to live, not to give in to that Bertram. Your body did what you told it to do to save your ass. The moment you realized you weren't shark chum, that twisted mind of yours decided to shave a couple years off our lives. You're not suicidal, but you're crazy-ass-wild, you know that?"

When he howled in laughter, I couldn't help but join him. After a breath, he said, "Maybe you're right."

"Which part?"

Henry settled back in his chair, appearing to have said all he wanted. Watching the blazing red sun disappear quietly into the darkening Atlantic I wondered, what made him so sad?

sixteen

The Long Girls

Clyde was first up, pumped for the day ahead. It was Friday, and the Long girls were coming. Henry had said they were scheduled to arrive at Harkers today, and he was supposed to pick them up.

Clyde had developed a fondness for Caroline last summer and was excited to see her again. Ready to get the day started, he walked over to the dresser and turned up the radio. A sportscaster was running on and on about Reggie Jackson's 10 RBIs in the A's win over the Red Sox, 21-7.

"What time is it?" John grumbled.

"It's daytime. Get out of the rack and let's get going," Clyde said. "Henry, what time did you say your mom and the girls arrive at Harkers?"

"Around lunchtime," Henry responded.

"I think you're excited, brother," I said.

"Yeah, a little."

"Oh really?" John cracked. "We hadn't noticed."

"Well John, I saw you smile a little when Henry said Mil was coming."

John grinned, "Yeah, she's cute."

"Soulful Strut" by Young-Holt Unlimited was playing in the background when I said, "We've got time before they arrive. Let's do some Jeep-skiing this morning. There's hardly a ripple out there."

Loaded on the Jeep, John threw it into four-wheel drive, and blasted over the sand dune beside the house to the sound. Clyde and I secured ropes to the Jeep and Henry jumped out, surfboard and rope in hand. When he was out as far as he could get, he called to John for a slow start. From his knees to his feet, all in one smooth motion, Henry was cutting, carving, and calling for more speed. He had it mastered on his first run.

At the old shipwreck close to Sally and Les's place, John slowed to a stop and Henry bailed to turn and start again.

"Mind if I join you?" I yelled to Henry.

"Hey, that sounds cool, let's try it."

I swam out as far as I could pull my rope and yelled over to Henry to call for the start. We figured out how to zig, when the other zagged and were soon locked in. Henry quickly mastered surfing across any choppy wake I left with my ski. Clyde followed me and added some more tricks.

We were having a blast trying new things at the edges of our abilities and beyond. The *beyond's*, with the hilarious wipeouts, were as much fun as the triumphs. We became so absorbed we lost track of time, until Clyde called in. Pulling my watch from between the seats I shouted, "Oh crap," it's eleven-thirty."

We packed it in and raced off to the dock. There was no time to get to Henry's boat. We'd have to bring the entire crowd back in the Whirlwind.

Our trip to Harkers was fast over the flat sound. Pulling into the marina we saw no signs of the Long girls. Backing into the slip, I said, "Clyde why don't you and Henry run up to the store? We'll take care of the boat."

"Thanks." He smiled big and trotted off with Henry.

John and I secured the Whirlwind and joined them with Mr. Credle at the drink cooler.

"Guess you've heard we're expecting some very important guests anytime now," I said to Mr. Credle.

"I don't think Clyde's taken his eyes off the driveway since he got here," Mr. Credle said with a wink.

"Sorry Mr. Credle, They are very cute."

At that moment, we heard a car enter the gravel driveway. Clyde's reaction left no doubt.

"It's them."

We filed out the door to greet them, as Clyde struggled to improve his position in line. Duna and Jane, ages eight and ten, jumped from the car and took off running for the dock, shouting something about boats and water.

Clyde and John were first to greet Caroline and Mil as they got out of the car. Henry and I said hello to Henry's mom, June Long and Henry's Aunt Mildred Long.

"We're going over in the Reeves' boat," Henry said to his mom.

"That sounds good, is our's OK?"

"It's just fine. The Whirlwind was closer when we noticed the time."

"Well, I'm glad you remembered us," Aunt Mildred said with a smile.

Henry, gesturing toward Clyde and John, said, "Those two haven't let us forget you . . . or *them,*" pointing to Caroline and Mil. "I've been staying with the guys at the A-Frame the last several days."

Lowering the tailgate to the station wagon, Henry began pulling out bags of vegetables, groceries, and clothes. I pulled a cart around from behind the marina store and started loading.

"Little help here boys?" Henry called to John and Clyde.

Eager to impress the girls, they began pulling out bags from the back, competing to see who could carry more to the boat.

"Come on girls, this way," Clyde said, unable to hide his enthusiasm.

Henry and I smiled at each other as we watched Clyde and John vie for the driver's seat. John used his size and Clyde, his agility. In the end, it was John with the prize.

Clyde quickly turned defeat into victory when he eased himself between Caroline and Mildred on the stern seat.

Once we were underway, Henry called across the boat to me to say, "We will hit bottom in this boat a long way from shore. Let's pull our boat out and float the ladies and gear ashore in it."

"Sounds good. Any oysters on the way?"

"No, just deep mud and lots of periwinkles."

When the Whirlwind's outboard started kicking up muck, John shut it off. Clyde paused his courting long enough to raise the outboard. Henry and I jumped over the side to get his boat. No one noticed. They were too busy in laughter and conversation.

Once we had the boats together, we began transferring ladies and gear to the shallow-draft boat.

Mrs. Long said, "Boys, we'd love for you to join us for supper tonight.

We looked at each other and Henry said, "That'd be great. We'd love it."

Caroline and Mil smiled big, and the little girls giggled.

Why don't y'all plan to come over around five to help?" Mrs. Long said.

"Perfect. It'll be good to get a hot meal. Now, let's get you ladies moved in."

We turned the gas back on, relit pilot lights, and pumped water. Henry gave a thumbs up when he was sure that everything was working properly, and we headed for the boat. The tide had fallen enough while we were at the cottage that we had to push a good thirty yards for enough water to motor away.

Back at the A-Frame, Henry and I sent Clyde and John to the showers to get pretty for the girls. We took care of the gear and straightened up the shed while they preened. By the time we finished quick showers, the Jeep was running with the two of them yelling for us to hurry up. Still wet and half dressed, we slid down the steel banister of the back stairs and jumped into the back. John shot off before our butts landed on the seat wells.

"Why such a hurry John?" Henry asked. "Afraid the girls'll find somebody better?"

"Very funny."

Turning onto the road to the Long cottage, the Rolling Stones' "Jumpin' Jack Flash" blasted. Clyde couldn't resist hopping onto the front of the Jeep for a little hood-surfing. Henry crawled over the front seat and joined him. The two bounced and twisted with the Jeep's gyrations and the song's rhythms. I did my best just to stay in my seat.

"Speed up!" Clyde shouted.

John instantly obliged. Some of the bumps launched them a foot off the hood, but they managed to stay aboard, all the way into the cottage drive. Jane and Duna, playing in the yard, squealed with delight when they saw them. Clyde and Henry topped off their show by jumping off well before the Jeep came to a stop. The commotion brought Caroline and Mil out the back door.

Mrs. Long was busy readying the grill. "Welcome boys, you're just in time to help. This corn needs shucking, and the veggies need attention. The girls will get you started at the picnic table."

Caroline had already put Clyde to work shelling a large bucket of peas. Everyone squeezed together to fit on the benches. Henry and I placed a couple of chairs at the ends.

In moments we were all happily snapping, shelling, and shucking.

"Are you girls all settled into the cottage?" Henry asked.

"Yes, Caroline said with a bright smile. "We're ready for fun."

"Hey," looking at Caroline and Mil, Clyde asked, "do y'all want to go skiing tomorrow?"

"That sounds great," Caroline said.

Mil nodded enthusiastically and said, "We're in."

"Fantastic. We'll pick you up tomorrow at nine at the Coast Guard dock," Clyde beamed.

Vegetables finished, Caroline and Mil went into the kitchen to help Aunt Mildred with the cooking. We called over to June to ask how we could help.

"Start the generator and open any closed shutters would be helpful."

Clyde turned to Henry and said, "I'll help you with the generator."

"John and I'll handle the shutters." We found that the shutter latches were stiff with salt and corrosion. With a little oil, applied by me, and force, by John, each one eventually opened.

The aromas coming from the kitchen and grill delivered on their promise. Mrs. Long's BBQ chicken dinner was delicious. We devoured it as fast as our Cape-degraded manners allowed. Following cleanup, we moved to the front porch.

On the way through the house, I overheard June say to Henry. "I know it's been rough since January, how are you doing out here?"

Duna and Jane's laughter in the hall drowned out Henry's response. *How was he doing? He hadn't been himself since we first saw him.*

The screen porch of the Long cottage was one of my favorite places on the Cape. There was plenty of room for large groups to gather and share colorful tales well into the night. Caroline and Mil were strategic in their seating, allowing spaces that Clyde and John quickly filled. Jane and Duna landed headlong onto the open sofa.

Caroline, Mil, Clyde, and John told stories from their earliest memories of the Cape until a little after nine when Aunt Mildred said, "It's been a busy day girls, time to call it a night."

"Yes ma'am" they all responded, almost in unison.

Standing up, John said, "We'll meet y'all at nine at the Coast Guard dock."

"You won't have to wait for us," Mil responded eagerly. "We'll be there."

We thanked June and Aunt Mildred for dinner and headed into the starry night for the A-Frame. Clyde and John were quiet on our ride back, just staring ahead or at the stars.

seventeen
A Near Sinking

Clyde shattered the morning's calm with Hugo Montenegro's "The Good, the Bad, and the Ugly." No obscenities followed.

"I can't wait to see those girls ski," Clyde said.

"They're good," Henry said. "They've been at it since they could walk."

Following a quick breakfast, we were off to the boat.

As John would be busy entertaining and skiing, I took the boat-driving duties for the day. The tide was extra high with the full moon, so I drove full speed across the bight heading straight for the Coast Guard dock. Looking toward the Long cottage, I spotted a car pulling from behind the house.

"The girls are leaving the cottage, and fast. They're excited to see you two."

"Not more than I am," Clyde whooped from the stern. "Remember to watch for submerged pilings where the old Coast Guard dock was. With this high tide, they're all underwater now."

"Got it," I said. "Pretty sure they're over there."

"I think Clyde's right," John said, "We're too close."

"OK," I said, feeling a little over-coached. "I'll slow down and move right."

Just then, the girls pulled up and started running down the dock in their tiny bikinis, with their white-blonde hair flying in the breeze.

Clyde and John were focused entirely on them. Suddenly, a sickening crack and violent lunge to starboard shattered the moment. Henry grabbed Clyde to keep him in the boat. John grabbed Clyde to stay in the boat.

"What the hell?"

Clyde dove for the deck and threw open the hatch. A geyser of water shot feet into the air and onto the deck. We had a basket-ball-sized hole in the bottom of our boat and a jagged piling sticking up through it. We were sinking – and fast.

"Everybody lean out as far as you can on the gunnel," Clyde screamed. "Maybe we can lift her off the piling."

The boat did lift, slowly at first. Then with a loud scraping sound and lurch, we were free. I backed away from the piling and the dock.

"If we stay on this side of the boat, we can keep the hole mostly above water," Clyde said.

Henry shouted up to the dock, "Girls, we'll have to do this another day."

"Good luck," they yelled.

The bilge pump shot a stream of water like a fountain off the high side. John dived into the stern compartment and rooted furiously through the clutter until he pulled out a bailing bucket. Henry climbed around me when he spotted a cooler under the bow and quickly joined the bailing effort. Clyde remained in the bilge, keeping the pump free of splinters and trash.

With an eye on the hole, I turned toward Harkers Island and worked the throttle to find the best speed and pitch to keep the incoming water to a manage-able flow. With some speed, Clyde pulled the stern plug for more water to drain.

Despite our best efforts, water poured in faster than we could throw it out. Clyde crawled under the bow and emerged with a couple of torn life jackets. He stuffed them into the hole, and with his bare feet, kicked them deeply into the jagged opening. The water flow slowed considerably.

"Nice work Clyde," Henry shouted. "You might have just saved our asses."

"That's until Dad finds out about this," John said.

Feeling lousy, I said, "Let me worry about that when we get this boat on dry land."

A torrent of worst-possible outcomes flooded my mind as we floundered our way to Harkers. Thankfully, I could mark the shallows off my list. With the high tide, we could maintain speed through the turns.

Yelling loudly enough to be heard over the motor and bailing, I said, "When we get inside the marina, we'll have to slow down to steer around the docks and boats. When that hole submerges, the pressure's gonna blow Clyde's patch. We might sink before we can get this thing on the trailer."

Henry shouted, as he bailed, "Pull me alongside the breakwater and I'll jump out and get Mr. Credle. We'll get the trailer in the water before you enter the marina."

"That's a good idea," John said. "Clyde, I'll trade places with you on the patch. I can hold it down better."

"I think we've got a plan," I said as I steered straight for the marina wall. When we neared the entrance, I slowed to run along the exterior wall for Henry to jump. Without regard for the splintering, barnacled pilings, he leapt for the top, made a firm grab, and pulled himself over to the deck on the other side. He was quickly in a full run toward the office.

Moments later, the two of them were in the Green Machine racing around to the back of the motel for the trailer. Just as fast, they returned and backed it down the ramp with amazing agility and speed.

On their signal, I headed into the marina's entrance. "Here we go boys. Pray we can keep this baby off the bottom."

Inside the breakwater, I slowed at the last possible moment to make the first turn around the outermost dock. As soon as I did, water shot up through the patch. John moved his foot to cover it, and two more springs shot up. Clyde bailed as fast as he could, but the bubbly white water poured across the deck like a fire hydrant had been opened. Steering became increasingly difficult as the boat sank deeper into the water. John's weight to hold the patch down diminished as more of him went underwater.

Clyde gave up bailing and yelled, "Lord, keep us afloat."

With the last turn made, I lined up on the trailer. Worried the motor would quit when the battery went under water, I bumped the throttle for one last push. The momentum was enough to shove us onto the trailer. With more throttle, the boat lunged closer to the wench, Mr. Credle yelled, "That's good."

"We made it," John screamed.

Over my pounding heart and our crew's shouts of celebration, the clicking of the wench pulling our Whirlwind the last few feet onto her trailer was sweet music.

John, Clyde, and I climbed over the side into the water on the ramp.

"We did it," Clyde said as the commotion calmed.

"Let's try to get her out of the water and see what damage you boys have done." Mr. Credle looked anxious as he headed for the truck.

Following a pop of the emergency brake and a racing motor, all four of the Green Machine's tires began to yank and squawk, struggling for a grip on the wet concrete ramp. Slowly, but surely, the truck began to pull our boat from the edge of her watery grave.

Reaching the top of the hill Mr. Credle stopped. We all dived under the boat to see the damage. The gash was considerably larger than what we'd thought from above. It ran a couple of feet and was more than a foot wide at its center. Seawater poured out like a small waterfall.

The spectacle had captured the attention of everyone in the motel and marina. No one, especially the old salts, could believe we'd made it all the way from the Cape with such a breach. Relief and satisfaction washed away the terror I'd kept stuffed down during our hour-long ordeal. *Thank you, Lord, for bringing us home.*

That boat continued to drain for the next hour we spent driving up and down the Island Road looking for a boat builder to repair the Whirlwind – hopefully for a reasonable price. Heading back toward the marina, about ready to give up, Clyde spotted a sign that hadn't been visible on our westward leg. "Hey, let's try Rose Brothers."

Pulling into the driveway, we saw a skinny old man coming down the ladder of a large sport fisherman under construction. We parked and walked his way.

In heavy Harkers brogue, he asked, "Can I help you boys?"

I held out my hand and said, "We hope so sir. I'm Sam Bass."

"I'm Cap'n Benny. Pleased to meet you." Looking at our leaking boat, he said, "What you got here?"

"I poked a hole in her and hope you can fix it."

He scratched his chin as he looked up and down the length of the hull, then a little longer at the gaping hole.

"Yep, you hurt her feelings pretty bad." How in the world did you keep her off the bottom?"

Before we could answer, he asked, "By the way, do you boys know what time it is?"

"It's a little past four-thirty."

"My Lord, Son of David, I have missed the 'Edge of Night.'"

We looked at each other, baffled. When he regained his composure, he knelt down and surveyed the damage once again.

"This is not too bad, boys, we can have her back in the water in a few days, probably by Thursday. Will that be alright?"

"Wow," I said, "that would be great! Thank you so much, where should we leave her? I asked.

"Over there, beside the shed door" he answered.

With our boat safely in the hands of a master, we headed back to the marina.

"What the heck is 'an edge of night?'" Clyde asked.

"It's a TV soap opera," Henry chuckled. "Some guys at school watched it."

We met Mr. Credle back at the marina and returned his keys. "Looks like you found someone to repair your boat."

I answered "Yessir, Cap'n Benny. He said he'd have her ready by Thursday."

"That's the best you could hope for," Mr. Credle said.

"Dad says Rose Brothers is one of the best boat builders on the east coast," Clyde said.

"That would be hard to argue. You boys will need a way back to the Cape. Take one of the rental skiffs. There's not much demand until Friday." Smiling he said, "Try not to punch any holes in her."

"Yessir," Clyde answered. You take mighty good care of us."

"Happy to do it. Boys, I'm real impressed with the way you brought that boat back. Most people would've panicked and let her sink, right there on the spot. I'm betting you've learned a lesson about sunken pilings too," winking, with a smile.

"Yessir, we have," Clyde said. "But just to make sure, Sam will not be driving your boat."

Everybody laughed, with a little more enthusiasm than I thought was fair, but I joined them, ecstatic it hadn't been worse.

We took the last skiff in the row, leaving the closer ones for paying customers. John sat in the stern, as skipper. He gave the gas bulb a few squeezes, a couple sharp yanks on the starter cord, and the twenty-five horse-power outboard sputtered to life, in a puff of blue smoke. I untied her bow, and we were off for the Cape.

Pulling out of the marina basin, Clyde said, "You know, we shouldn't leave this boat in the water tonight. She could swamp in a heavy thunderstorm."

Henry said, "We beach ours above the high tide mark and leave an anchor out."

"That's good thinking, we don't want to sink another one," John said.

"Guys, I'm really sorry for ruining our day. And thanks for saving my ass. It would have been mighty hard to tell Uncle Charlie and Dad that I'd sunk the Whirlwind."

"We weren't saving *your* ass. We were saving *our* boat," John teased.

"Well, either way, we sure pulled together today, like a team to stay afloat."

"The CLSU lives to fight another day," Clyde shouted proudly.

John, Clyde, and I shouted and threw our fists into the breeze.

Looking at Henry, I said, "A few years back, we called ourselves the CLSU, for Cape Lookout Survival Unit. We painted the letters on some Army helmets we got in Fayetteville. They probably saved our lives when we broke the Jeep in half dune-jumping."

"We didn't have to tell Dad we'd sunk the Jeep when Clyde welded it back together," John said, patting Clyde on the shoulder.

Smiling, Clyde said, "We had our own fort too when we dug the sand out of the gun mounts. They've filled in with some, but you can still crawl around in them."

"I'd like to check that out," Henry said.

Our little skiff glided smoothly across the calm Back Sound. The breeze was cool, and the sunlight had softened to a light golden hue. The beauty of the water, the dunes, and the drone of our little engine was calming after our near catastrophe. *Thank you, Lord. I don't deserve it but thank you.*

A few minutes later, Clyde said, "Henry, since we couldn't take the girls skiing today, let's invite them for a beach day tomorrow."

"Sounds fun," Henry replied. "John, you can shoot straight across the bight. This skiff doesn't draw more than a foot of water."

As we pulled the boat onto the shore, the entire household emptied onto the front yard to welcome us. We were quickly on the screen porch with Clyde recounting the story with his usual flare.

At its conclusion, Mrs. Long looked at me, with a reassuring smile and said, "Sam, it could have happened to anybody. It's a mess over there. Boys, I'm mighty proud of all of you for saving that boat. Well done."

"Thank you, Mrs. Long. I sure hope our fathers feel the same way," I said.

Looking at Caroline and Mil, Clyde asked, "Do you want to have a beach day tomorrow?"

"That sounds like fun," Caroline said, and Mil quickly agreed.

"Would you mind taking Duna and Jane along too?" Mrs. Long asked.

"We'd love to have them," Henry said. The girls squealed with delight.

"We'll see you tomorrow about nine," Henry said as we headed back to our little boat, and the A-Frame.

Eighteen

Beach Days

Clyde and John were first to stir and wasted no time getting out the door after breakfast. Henry and I packed some sandwiches, drinks, and water while they loaded the boards onto the flatbed. We were still munching pop tarts as we climbed into the Jeep. Reaching the landing strip, John floored it with little concern for riders or boards. We held onto them with one hand and our lives with the other.

"There're the girls." Clyde pointed toward the beach.

John yanked the wheel hard over, almost throwing Henry and me off the back. Without slowing, he bounded across the beach throwing us and the boards high into the air. It was a welcome relief when he stopped, beside the girls.

Caroline grinning, said, "We couldn't wait and decided to meet you out here."

"That's great," Clyde said. "Let's get in the water."

The girls didn't try to hide their excitement as they all eagerly climbed aboard the flatbed.

The waves were short, and slow to break making them perfect for Duna and Jane." Clyde cranked up "Pipeline" by the Ventures as the truck rolled to a stop at the high-tide berm.

Caroline and Mil jumped off, grabbed their boards, and bounded off into the surf. Over their shoulders they yelled, "Come on dudes – surf's up." They were beautiful and full of energy. Running as far as they could through the breakers, they hit their boards and paddled out to ride the next wave in. Jane and Duna grabbed their boogie boards and followed their sisters.

Clyde was next and John wasn't far behind.

"Do you mind helping me keep an eye on the little girls?" Henry asked.

"Not at all. There's not much surf yet anyway."

"Yeah," Henry agreed.

The little girls screamed with every takeoff on the foamy waves. None of the Long girls held anything back. They fed off the challenge of outdoing each other, trick by trick. It was a family trait.

John, Mil, Caroline, and Clyde rode a few, then settled into conversations on their boards beyond the break.

"Looks like our surfers have gotten pretty particular with their wave selection. Waves aren't the only thing going on out there," I said.

"They do seem distracted, or is it *attracted?* Henry chuckled.

After a couple of hours, Duna and Jane ambled up, dragging their boogie boards behind. Henry and I had laid a long board in the sand and loaded it up with the sandwiches, melons, and drinks that Mrs. Long had sent.

The girls pounced on the spread. In a raised voice Henry said, "Woah, girls. This food's for all of us. You're acting more like seagulls, than little ladies."

Giggling, they curbed their frenzy and said, 'Yes sir.'

"Uncle Henry, when are you and Sam going in?" Jane asked.

"Soon. We're your lifeguards until Mil and Caroline come in for lunch. We'll go out then. Girls, this is important. Ya'll need to be out of the water when there's no one up here watching you. Do you understand?"

"Yessir," they said, nodding with crinkled lips and brows.

Jane and Duna finished their sandwiches when Caroline and Clyde ran up, followed by Mil and John.

"The waves aren't great, but they're fun," Caroline said.

Reaching for a sandwich, Clyde warned, "Henry, you'd better watch out for these cousins of yours."

BOYS ON THE EDGE

"Don't I know it," Henry answered. "And don't worry about the waves guys. Small craft warnings are up for the afternoon, with winds out of the east-south-east. That'll give us a perfect break." Looking at Duna and Jane, he said, "You girls should probably go back out now, before it gets too rough."

With squeals of joy and "Yessirs" they gulped down what was left of their lunch and ran back into the water.

After an hour or so, the chop was bad enough for Henry to call the girls in.

"OK Uncle Henry, can we have just one more ride?" Duna pleaded.

"Yes, then come on in."

Following a good long ride, they came in just as they'd promised.

"You girls are getting better and better. You'll be as good as your big sisters before you know it," Henry said. "Get a big drink of water before you head back for the cottage. And wear your flip flops."

'Yes sir,' they giggled.

We had started waxing our boards when Jane asked, "Uncle Henry, can we stay and watch?

"Sure. Just head home when you get tired."

Henry and I ran into the waves to join the others beyond the brake. The sun was hot, the waves were building with a strong undertow. When I neared Clyde and Caroline, I asked, "How is it?"

"Much better now," Caroline answered.

"OK girl – school's in – teach us something," Henry said.

"You're on."

She grinned and paddled off. She was on the next wave. It was a good one. She dropped in smoothly and took a sharp bottom turn back up the face. With speed she did a few carves, throwing some spray over the back of the wave. She climbed to the wave's shoulder, took a steep turn, all the way around, for a perfect 180 to escape the foam. It was fun to watch, including the awesome wipeout finish. Shaking it off, she eagerly paddled back out to us.

"That was a beautiful roundhouse cutback. The crash was nice too," Henry smiled.

"Where's that been hiding?" Clyde asked.

Grinning, she said, "I was waiting for some juice."

Henry chuckled and said, "You mean some audience."

"No," she protested.

"Well Henry, I guess you're on – with a tough act to follow," I said.

"Yep, she set a good mark," Henry yelled as he dug in to catch the next wave. He was up fast and took a hard bottom turn up to the wave's shoulder. On the top, he did a perfect 'off-the-lip' spin, which is a vertical 180 degree turn that starts with half the board out above the wave and ends with the surfer heading back down the wave.

At the base, he made another sharp turn back up the wave to its shoulder and did a 'floater,' riding his board sideways along the top of the wave, fins out on the back side. When the wave started closing, he did a prone kick-out, to land on his belly and paddle back our way. We clapped and hooted loudly.

We continued the afternoon surfing individually and in groups, as the waves allowed. We even took a few party waves, where the whole group rides together, close enough to talk to each other.

The rising tide and larger waves made conditions increasingly dicey. Henry was a risk-taker, but not with his cousins.

"We'd better call it a day. The waves are starting to close on the beach. We don't want any broken bones or teeth."

All agreed and we headed in and saw that Duna and Jane had left for the cottage. After stacking the boards on the truck bed, we sat in the shade of the truck and finished off the drinks and food. Tunes played in the background as Caroline and Mil shared highlights from their cheerleading, swim, and tennis teams.

Swallowing a bite of peach, Clyde said, "Hey, why don't y'all come over to the A-Frame tonight? We can grill some hamburgers and show you the house."

"That sounds like fun," Caroline answered, "but I'm sure mom will want Jane and Duna to come along too." Mil agreed.

"That's OK," John said. "They'll have fun too."

When the truck's shadow reached the water's edge, we called it a day and headed back to the Long cottage, Mil beside John, and Clyde, beside Caroline. Henry and I entertained ourselves with a little hood surfing.

At the cottage, Clyde and John went straight in with the girls. "Mom," Mil said, "the boys invited us to the A-Frame tonight for games and hamburgers. We'll take Duna and Jane along with us. Can we go?"

"That sounds wonderful" Aunt Mildred quickly responded, more eagerly than we expected. "We have some leftover corn and beans we'll send with you."

"Thanks," Clyde said. "We'll be back in an hour or so to pick y'all up."

On the way back to the A-Frame, John and Clyde discussed ideas of how to entertain their guests.

"There's a new badminton set in the garage," Clyde said.

"The beach in front of the house is loaded with shells and sand dollars for Duna and Jane," John added.

"What about y'all walking them to the lighthouse, while Henry and I cook the burgers?"

"That's a great idea," Clyde said. "Y'all don't mind?"

"You boys show my cousins some fun and leave the rest to us."

When we got to the house, Clyde and John unloaded the flatbed and headed for the showers. Henry and I readied the kitchen, the grill, and started defrosting the burgers. After pouring a bag of charcoal, I went back into the kitchen and found Henry banging around for a couple of pots for the vegetables.

"This is going to be fun," I said. Too bad we don't have dates too."

"Yep. Hey, are there any buns for the burgers?"

Uh . . . yeah, I'm sure there're a couple of bags in the freezer. I'll get 'em."

After a noticeably long freshening-up, John and Clyde came down the stairs, hair combed, wearing their best cutoff jeans and collared shirts.

"Wow," Henry exclaimed, "I'd better go along to introduce you two."

"Very funny," John sneered, as they walked out the back door. Henry and I followed them out.

Unable to hide their smiles, they jumped into the truck, spun tires, and threw sand high into the air as they raced off to fetch their dates.

Looking at Henry, I said in a sappy tone, "They grow up so fast, don't they?"

Henry chuckled, turned, and headed into the kitchen. I walked through the house and grabbed the radio on my way to the front corner of the deck. It had become my refuge. The ocean breeze was cool, and the light was golden-soft with the sun setting over Atlantic Beach. Three Dog Night's "One" played quietly on the radio. One *was* a lonely number. What would life be like alone?

While pondering the question of loneliness, "Love Can Make You Happy," by Mercy came on. The song had become a favorite of mine – a fact I kept to myself. As the lyrics rolled, I hoped there was someone out there for me love. Someone who made me happy and could give a lifetime to me. I was falling in love with the idea of love. There was no someone.

The clatter of the Jeep engine in the distance snapped me out of my musing. I yelled through the front screen door to Henry. "They'll be here in a couple of minutes.

"We'll be ready," Henry said.

"I'll start the charcoal when they leave for the lighthouse."

Through the back screen door, we heard the group singing "Sweet Caroline" at the top of their lungs. I later learned the song was a family favorite.

Duna and Jane came bounding up the steps and Jane asked, "Can we see the house?"

"Of course," I said, "help yourselves, but be careful on the stairs, they're steep.

"Hello Uncle Henry," they shouted as they ran through the kitchen. They were on the third floor in no time, poking their heads out the latticed openings and yelling down to the living room below.

"Be careful girls, don't stick any more than your heads out. Don't want to have to catch you," Henry yelled.

"Yessir," they answered, squealing as they jumped on the beds, looked through the portholes, and opened and slammed closet and bathroom doors.

The foursome entered next, with John starting his tour. Mil and Caroline were wide-eyed as they emerged from the hallway and saw the glass windows of the 'A' showcasing the beautiful afternoon sky.

"Here's the kitchen, obviously. On the left, is Mom and Dad's bedroom. Go on in, take a look."

John followed them in as they studied the queen bed, dresser, and small seating area on the way to the private bath. Caroline said, "What luxury." Then she pointed to the stack of cardboard boxes against the front louvered wall, marked 'US Army.' "What are those?"

Clyde jumped in, "They're our dinners when we don't feel like cooking. They're C-Ration food kits, used by soldiers in Vietnam. Dad brought them out here when he and John's brothers were building the A-Frame, and they couldn't cook.

Later, as their tour was wrapping up, I suggested, "Guys, why don't you go see the lighthouse now, before it gets dark. The girls can collect shells and chase sand crabs along the way. We'll have dinner ready by the time you get back."

"That sounds fun," Mil answered. "They've been asking to see the lighthouse."

"The Coast Guard lets us climb it when the door's open, but it's probably locked up by now. If you do climb it tonight, remember that the stair treads are tall and wide open. Jane and Duna could easily slip right through. Hold onto them," I said.

Mil acknowledged, then turned toward the tall sand dune beside the house to say, "Girls, do you want to go see the lighthouse?"

"Yes," they squealed, dropping their game of Queen on the Mountain.

They were quickly off. Duna and Jane ran all over the beach and circled the teens like mosquitoes. The wind was blowing pretty briskly by now, so I pulled the grill around to the back corner of the house, to cook in the lee. Pouring an ample amount of kerosine over the coals, I went into the kitchen to get some matches, giving the fuel time to saturate the coals. Henry was just finishing seasoning the burgers with garlic salt, pepper, and Worcester sauce.

"The coals will be ready in about fifteen minutes. Want to shoot for dinner in about thirty? Everybody's probably starved after our day on the waves."

"Yea sounds OK." Henry said.

I took the radio out to the grill. The DJ slowed things down with "This Guy's In Love with You," by Herb Albert, and "My Special Angel," by the Vogues.

I had just taken the burgers off the grill and was toasting some buns when I heard them walking up. I yelled through the kitchen porthole to let Henry know they were back.

When the little girls came bounding up the steps. I sent them into the downstairs bathrooms to wash their hands.

"How was it?" I asked the four.

"It was really neat," Mil answered. "It's been a long time since I've been to the lighthouse and the Keeper's house. Unfortunately, they were all locked up."

"We'll go up next time the guys are doing maintenance," Clyde said.

"Supper's ready," I said while lifting the last of the buns off the fire. Sounds of amazement came from the group as I turned toward them with the burgers and buns. When I got to the screen door, I saw why. The front windows of the A-Frame looked like a cathedral's stained glass windows. They glowed bright orange and red clouds as the sun's rays bathed the pine walls in golden light. The row of lanterns looked like candles, adding to the cathedral-like feel.

Gathering around the kitchen counter, our group was quiet. I said, "Let's say a blessing." Heads bowed, I continued, "Dear God, we thank you for this great day, this beautiful place, and this food. Most of all, thank you for keeping us safe today and our boat afloat yesterday. Amen."

Laughter and conversations resumed as we went through the line, youngest first.

"We're leaving Friday," Mil said.

"Oh no, feels like you just got here," John responded, sadly.

"Yeah, we're going to cheerleading camp. It runs until school starts."

"Well, we'll have to cram everything in these next couple of days," Clyde said emphatically.

"That's a deal." Caroline smiled.

After dinner, we gathered around the coffee table for some ghost stories. Duna and Jane seemed a little bored, so I threw out an idea. "Why don't we continue this at the old, haunted house in the maritime forest?"

The little ones loved the idea and Mil said, "That could be fun. Let's do it."

We all crowded aboard the flatbed and were soon weaving our way along the sandy road. The entire island glowed bright white in the full moon. Mil and Caroline led us in singing camp songs like "If I Had a Hammer," "Row Your Boat," and O' Suzanna."

The lights around the Coast Guard station were all lit, but the concrete compound was quiet. We saw some of the men playing cards in the mess hall. Over the motor pool, a group stood around what we knew was a large pool table in the rec room. We idled through the drive, as was our custom, and *their* strict rule.

Beyond the station, the concrete road gave way to a grassy path that was the entrance to the maritime forest. The first cottage on the right belonging to the Styron family, was dark and empty. It was one of ten or so small, well-kept houses owned mostly by Down Eastern families. John slowed even further as the road grew darker under the dense canopy of live oaks. Rather than stop to see if the headlights were on, Clyde fumbled around for, and found a flashlight between the seats. He began sweeping its weak-orange beam from side-to-side to reveal the wooded borders of the road.

Tree tops swayed in the breeze above, but the air around us was still and damp. Earthy aromas of dank cedar, live oak, peat, and juniper filled the misty air. With each turn the forest grew darker and more foreboding. Duna and Jane, clinging tightly to their sisters, were no longer bored.

"Are we on the right road?" Clyde asked.

Henry said, "It should be just ahead on the left."

Pointing his light left, as Henry had directed, brought a collective gasp. There it stood, darker than the night, reaching high into the trees with its gothic arches and spires. Some of the upper-story shutters swung hauntingly in the breeze. The scant remaining red paint looked like glistening blood when Clyde's flashlight hit it.

"Doesn't look much like the Coca-Cola house tonight," Clyde said quietly.

John pulled into the yard and turned off the engine. The only sounds that could be heard were squeaking shutters and a few chirping crickets. Henry hopped off the truck, took the flashlight from Clyde, and looking at me said, "Come on."

When we stepped onto the rough wood and protruding nails on the front porch, I wished I had worn my flip flops.

"Come on guys," Henry said, shining the light behind us at the truck.

The group reluctantly hopped off and joined us on the porch. The little girls were startled by the squeaking of the screen door. I held it open for everyone to file through and gather inside the porch. Henry grasped the front doorknob, gave it a turn and a bump with his shoulder. With a scuff over the threshold, the door opened by a few inches. The rusty hinges moaned hauntingly when he pushed the door open further to sweep the room with the flashlight to ensure we would be the only ones in the room.

"All clear," he said to the sound of a few sighs of relief.

The dusty, wide-planked floors creaked under the weight of each footstep. Cobwebs covered the old brass chandelier in the center of the grand living room, and they filled every corner. The tall windows were too dusty and painted to let in any light, had there been any outside. The cold, still, darkness of the room nearly swallowed up the beam of Henry's flashlight.

"Who's up for a ghost story? He asked.

"Uncle Henry. This is too scary. Can we go home?" Duna's voice trembled and Jane nodded earnestly.

Mil's expression, seen in the flashlight's glow, left no doubt as to the answer.

"Of course. Maybe we'll come back in the daytime." Henry said.

"Not me." Jane said.

With that, everyone quickly exited the house and climbed aboard the flatbed, holding tightly to each other. John started the engine and raced down the path, with Clyde doing the best he could to light the way. Once out of the forest, the road and landscape were once again lit brilliantly by the moonlight. The little girls' spirits lifted when they saw the cottage ahead.

Before we entered the house, Duna and Jane had told their scary story to Aunt June and their mother. When Clyde spoke up to apologize, Caroline said, "Girls, you can sleep with Mil and me tonight. We'll watch out for you."

Their reaction suggested they'd be fine.

Clyde said, "Let's do some sightseeing tomorrow. Maybe take the Jeep to the north end of Core Banks to Drum Inlet. There're some neat villages and sights along the way."

"The lighthouse might be open for a climb too," John said.

They nodded emphatically, and Caroline said, "We'll pack a picnic lunch."

Clyde, grinning ear to ear, said, "We'll pick you up after breakfast."

On the ride home I yelled out, "Boys, Henry and I think you're ready to take the family truck out on a date by yourselves. Take good care of her."

"And take care of my cousins," Henry shouted. "Clyde, I'm depending on you to keep an eye on John."

"Ha," John laughed. "You're the ladies' man, my friend."

"Just the same Clyde."

"You bet Henry. I'll keep him in line," Clyde shouted boldly.

The two discussed their plans for the rest of the ride back and into the evening, before calling it a night.

John was first to stir. He threw a pillow at Clyde, saying, "Rise and shine. Let's get an early start for a full day."

"Alright," Clyde mumbled, fighting off sleep. His enthusiasm quickly matched John's. "We're gonna have a great day."

Coming down the steps into the kitchen, I heard Clyde say, "Let's take an extra can of gas. The motor strains pretty hard in the deep sand up at the north end of the island."

"Good idea,"

"I'm gonna throw a slalom ski and rope in too – in case the ocean flattens out," Clyde said.

"Yeah, that'd be fun for the girls," Henry said with a wink.

Tossing their bowls into the sink, the two headed for the shed. Clyde turned. "See ya' boys. Don't wait up for us."

Henry grinned, then shouted, "Remember what I said last night Clyde."

"Don't worry Henry, we'll take good care of the girls." Minutes later, the Jeep fired up and they were off on their day-long island date.

"So, I was thinking, while the kids are away, why don't we take the skiff to Atlantic Beach to see what we might find," I said.

"Now that's a worthwhile idea. The Jolly Knave might have something going on. They'll be beach action anyway."

"Yea, I thought we'd cruise by a friend's cottage. There's usually a fun crowd there from Sanford."

After filling a couple of boat tanks with gasoline and outboard motor oil, we headed to the dock. The skiff sat at the water's edge just waiting for us.

"Wind's not bad, should be a pretty smooth ride. I'll drive us if you like," Henry said.

After exchanging the tanks for full ones, we pushed off and were on our way. The ocean's swells weren't small, but neither of us showed any concern as we raced along in our ten-foot skiff. We figured we'd make Atlantic Beach in under an hour.

The sea oats and dunes rolled smoothly by with our little Evinrude running full speed. "Did you date much at VES?" I shouted over the motor's whine.

"I met a few local girls in Lynchburg and had the occasional date for football games, but pickins were slim."

"Well, slim pickins wasn't my problem. The girls I was interested in were interested only in junior and senior football players. Got real tired of the way they acted all superior and I just quit trying."

"Yeah, I guess it was nice starting fresh." Henry said.

"I met a girl earlier this summer, at the cottage we'll ride by. I fell big time for her, and she liked me too, but she had a boyfriend. I'm coming up empty this summer."

"Well, don't give up yet. There're prospects ahead – I know it."

I turned toward Atlantic Beach and let my thoughts drift. The sun was hot, and the salt spray cooled my face. With Fort Macon off our starboard, I yelled to Henry, "Steer close to the beach."

Riding the swells, a hundred yards off the beach, we saw a few groups of sunbathing girls, but no activity at the Perry cottage.

"I've got a good feeling about the Jolly Knave," Henry said. "We can come back this way if there's nothing going on there."

I nodded, and Henry twisted the throttle back to full speed. After rows and rows of cottages, we reached the Circle of Atlantic Beach. Just beyond it was the Jolly Knave. There was no activity on its front deck, but a group of four girls sat on the beach out front.

"Want to check 'em out?" Henry asked.

"Yeah, sure. It's why we're here."

He slowed to a stop, and I threw out the anchor. Moments later, we were over the side, swimming for the shore. Standing in the suds, we shook the water out of our hair and walked their way.

"Hey guys, welcome to Atlantic Beach. Are you lost?" the cutest of the four asked.

Henry stood up straight and said, "Hello lovelies. We've come all the way from Cape Lookout just to meet you." Bowing slightly, he said, "I'm Henry, this is Sam."

Nodding, I followed his lead. "Good morning, fair ladies. Might we learn your names?"

Our greeter started, "I'm Lisa. Meet Wendy, Karen, and Beth."

"Hello, can we join you?" Henry asked.

"Sure," Karen said, opening the cooler, "Would you like a drink?"

We sat on the beach, between them and the water and were soon sharing our hometowns, interests, and summer activities. They were fascinated by the idea of our living alone for the summer on the Cape. They were down for the week, staying at Lisa's parents' beach house.

"Hey, do y'all want to come out to the Cape for the day on Saturday? We can't get you all in that little skiff, but we get our big boat back tomorrow afternoon. We could pick you up Saturday morning."

"Oh wow, that sounds fun," Lisa said, "but my cousin's getting married this weekend, and we're in the wedding. We come down pretty often, can we come another time?"

157

"You bet," I said.

We enjoyed the afternoon, swapping stories and making plans to get together in a couple of weeks. When the sun was about three hours from the horizon, we said goodbye to our new feminine friends and headed home.

"I liked that Wendy. She was cute and funny," Henry said. "I hope she comes back with Lisa next week."

"Yeah, I thought Lisa was a doll. Fun to talk to.

Clyde and John rolled into the driveway just before sunset. Moments later they were in the kitchen, shower bound.

"Man, we had the best time today," Clyde beamed. The girls are so much fun. You should see how fast they took to Jeep skiing. We skied most of the way back."

"They want us to join them for supper tonight, so you guys get ready," John said.

"Don't we look ready?" Henry teased. "We've had our showers, but I guess we'd better comb our hair and press our jackets. We'll be ready."

On the ride to the Long cottage, Clyde shouted over the engine, "It's too bad the girls have to leave tomorrow. They're a lot of fun – very different fun than you guys are."

Henry and I smiled at each other.

nineteen

Wiley

"Welcome boys," June said as we walked into the kitchen. Aromas of frying chicken and mouth-watering biscuits filled the air. "We're so glad you could join us. We have all this chicken that needs to be eaten."

"The girls are putting the finishing touches on, but they seemed to have had a wonderful time with you, Clyde and John," Mildred said.

"We had a blast," John blurted, unable to hide his enthusiasm.

"Henry, what did you and Sam do with your day?" Mildred asked.

"We decided the skiff could use a little exercise, so we took a sea cruise to Atlantic Beach. We happened upon some lovely young ladies from Greenville and spent the afternoon entertaining them. Turns out they are beach regulars, so we expect to see them again."

"Well, I'm delighted to hear you had a good time son," June said.

John and Clyde, carrying out their duties of setting the table, nearly dropped the forks and plates when Mil and Caroline gracefully glided in, looking like they were ready for beach prom night.

"Wow," Clyde said.

"Wow," John said. "You girls look beautiful."

"Since it was our last night, we wanted to dress up a little," Mil said before her mom could say anything.

"We're glad you approve," Caroline said smiling with that cute crinkle in her nose.

"I don't think the Cape's ever seen finer," June said.

Dinner was delicious. Mil and John, Clyde, and Caroline, obviously hungry from their long day, struggled to eat while expounding upon and animating their favorites of the day. Following a quick cleanup with everyone helping, we made our way to the porch to hear more tales of the foursome's adventures.

June called for quiet when she heard something. We all recognized it as the distinctive drone of a single engine airplane approaching from the direction of the mainland. We followed Mrs. Long through the screen door to the front yard and she said, "It's your Uncle Wiley."

When he was overhead, very low to the ground, he shut off his engine, stuck his head out and yelled from under the wing, "June, what do you need?"

As calm as you please, June cupped her hands and yelled back, "Three breads, four dozen eggs, and coffee."

Wiley yelled back, "Got it, see you soon." He restarted his engine and circled back toward the mainland.

"He's going to Beaufort to get the groceries and he'll be back in a little while."

From our first encounter, Wiley Long had lived up to his legend as described by Henry, Les, Sally, Mr. Credle, and our parents. He was larger than life, especially in the air.

"Your husband is some pilot, Mrs. Long," Clyde said.

"I'll tell you a pilot story about Wiley Long. First, let's get inside before the mosquitoes carry us away."

As we settled into our seats Mrs. Long began. "Last year, Wiley and I were flying to a wedding in Myrtle Beach. Halfway into our trip, air traffic control warned of a powerful storm that had surprised forecasters. Wiley headed for the closest airport, but the storm overtook us. I was seated behind him and couldn't see or hear much that was going on. But out of my side window it looked like we were a tiny boat being tossed about on a stormy sea.

"Wiley was just as calm as ever. Next thing I knew, there were trees on either side of the plane. We weren't flying *over* them – we were falling *through* them. We hit the ground with a terrible jolt. Wiley yanked open the plane door and yelled – 'June get out.'

"Probably in shock, I looked at him and said, 'No way. I'm not leaving this dry plane to get out into that pouring rain and swamp.'"

"'June' he said, 'we've just crashed. There's the possibility of a gas leak and fire. It's protocol to abandon a crashed airplane as fast as you can.'

"'That may well be, but I don't smell any gasoline and I can't imagine a fire starting in this downpour. No, I'm not getting out, and that's final, Wiley Long.' So, we spent the night in our cozy little airplane.

"The next morning, rescuers woke us up, elated to find that we were alive. As they checked us for injuries, they told us three other planes had gone down in the storm – with no survivors. One was a military aircraft.

"I had no idea that we were in trouble, until after we were down. Wiley told me that the huge volume of rain had doused our engine. He used the storm's wind to lower the plane like a helicopter, through the trees, to the ground. Everyone was amazed how little damage there was to the plane. They had to take it apart to get it out of the forest. Yes, Wiley Long is quite a pilot!"

Hearing his plane in the distance, Mrs. Long said, "Henry, please go fetch your dad."

"Yes ma'am, Henry replied. Girls, do you want to come along? We'll take the Jeep too, so everyone can go."

Over Duna and Jane's squeals, Mrs. Long said, "OK, but y'all be careful."

"We will."

Heading out the door, Clyde, John, Caroline, and Mil hopped into the Jeep.

Duna and Jane followed Henry and me to the Olds. I had looked forward to riding in it since Henry told us his dad had brought it out. When I opened the door, the dome light actually came on. The chrome gleamed and the fabric seats oozed luxury.

"Henry, I feel like we should take another shower."

The girls had no such compunction, jumping quickly into the back seat, sandy feet, and all.

When Henry turned the key, I asked, "How do you know it's running?"

With a laugh he responded, "Know what you mean. The muffler hasn't had a chance to rust out yet. This baby's even got air conditioning and power brakes."

"Air conditioning?"

"Yeah, dad asked me to pull it out, but I haven't gotten around to it yet."

"Can we give it a try before you yank it? I've never felt air conditioning on the Cape."

Henry said, "Crank it up, and while you're at it, put some tunes on."

I obliged by turning the volume knob just beyond the click. When the warm yellow light of the dial came to life, I tuned it to WMBL. Steam's "Na Na Hey Hey, Kiss Him Goodbye" was playing. Henry urged some volume, so I happily twisted the dial near full, instantly impressed with the Old's sound system. The girls laughed and screamed while covering their ears. I yelled to Henry, "Man this system rocks! If your dad wants to pull out the radio too, let's put it in the Jeep."

Wasting no time, I reached for the air conditioner and turned it wide open. The cool air blasted into the car making for the most unfamiliar and incredible car ride ever on Cape Lookout. My tee shirt fluttered in the cool breeze as the powerful music rattled my bones. The soft ride on the shock absorbers and cushioned seats seemed surreal when Steppenwolf's, "Magic Carpet Ride" came on.

All was interrupted when Henry rolled his window down to check for his dad's approach. I turned off the radio, killed the A/C and rolled down my window to listen on my side.

"There he is," I yelled. "He's holding a flashlight out his window."

"Yeah, Henry said, he's checking for any surprises that might be on the field, like potholes, driftwood, or pilings. I scanned it when we rode in from the A-Frame and didn't see anything."

When Wiley had finished his pass down the field, he turned back toward the far end of the runway to land into what little wind there was. He slowed his motor to a near idle and dropped gently toward the field. Henry parked the car near where he'd tie the plane down.

Following a gentle touchdown, he taxied into the tie-down area that was surrounded on three sides by tall sand dunes. The prop was still spinning when he climbed out of the plane. We came up as he opened the cargo door. He pulled out some canvas straps and tossed them under each wing and the tail gear.

"Henry, tie her down for me, will you?"

As Henry went to work, we put the groceries and his duffel bag into the Olds' trunk.

Our trip back was considerably calmer than the ride to the airfield had been. At the cottage, June hugged her husband, pulled a warm plate heaped with fried chicken and vegetables out of the oven, and set it on the single place setting at the table.

We moved on to the porch for more stories. When Wiley joined us, John was describing how his dad usually announced his arrival, flying just a few feet off the roof of the A-Frame. Wiley got a kick hearing how the sheets sucked right off our beds.

"Mr. Long, when did you start flying? I asked.

"Well, that's a funny story. I got the bug as a young boy watching local barn-stormers do their tricks over our farm. Their landing field was close-by. One afternoon a pilot looked down and saw me waving to him. He landed in our pasture and took me for a ride. I was immediately hooked.

"Soon after that, the war started and I wanted to join up, but they didn't take me right away, so I went to Chapel Hill for college. During summer break, I told my father I wanted to be a pilot when the Army got around to taking me. He told me he would pay for my flying lessons at the Chapel Hill Airport, as long as they didn't interfere with my studies."

"What my father didn't share with me was that he told the flight instructor to scare me so bad that I wouldn't ever want to get in an airplane again. He'd seen so many pilots killed in the war, that he believed my odds would be far better on the ground. When that day came, that instructor did his level best to keep his promise to my old man. The more he dived, rolled, looped, and ran along the ground upside down, the louder I screamed for more."

All eyes were open wide as Wiley relived the excitement of his first flight. Clyde and I inched our chairs closer as he demonstrated the airplane's acrobatics with his hands and arms.

"Will you tell us what you did in the war?" Clyde asked.

"Well, they did finally call me up, about a year after I'd enlisted. Following flight school, they assigned me to a P51 fighter squadron to defend the heavy, slow-flying bombers on their missions into occupied Europe."

"Wow, I exclaimed, "you flew the P51 Mustang? That's my absolute favorite fighter."

Wiley sat up in his seat, and with renewed enthusiasm, said, "So you know something about that spectacular warbird. The Mustang was magnificent. She was powered by a Rolls Royce Merlin supercharged V12 engine and could do almost 450 miles per hour at high altitude.

"My early missions were flying fighter escort for the B-17 bombers, but we were so effective shooting down the Luftwaffe fighters, they soon stopped coming up to harass the bombers."

"No longer needed for escort duties, our missions changed to what the brass called 'targets of opportunity.' These were things like supply trains, munitions, and fuel depots.

"One afternoon on patrol, I spotted a Luftwaffe airfield with ten fully fueled, Messerschmitt B109's, five on each side of the field. With surprise on my side, I dropped in with the sun behind me and strafed the closest planes. After completing my run, I was curious why there hadn't been any anti-aircraft fire. Wondering how I'd gotten so lucky, I circled back and strafed the other five. Pulling up to get a better look, I saw seven of the ten in flames.

"Not wanting to push my luck, with low fuel and ammo, I headed home, hoping my nose camera caught all the action.

"Later that afternoon, lying in my bunk writing a letter back home, our squadron commander popped in and said, 'Boys, you have an ace in your midst. Lieutenant Wiley Long single-handedly wiped out seven top-line Messerschmitts 109s today.'

"He went on to say 'Lieutenant Long found himself in the right place at the right time. Turns out he caught the squadron with their pants down. Early that morning, they had moved their anti-aircraft guns to the new field thinking the planes would be safe under cover of a thick fog. But the lieutenant happened along just as the fog was lifting and the pilots were finishing their breakfast sausages."

The girls were talking among themselves quietly, but Clyde, John, Henry, and I remained riveted on Wiley's every word.

Were you ever shot down," Clyde asked.

Yes, but it looks like the ladies are getting bored. I'll tell you that story another time."

"Girls," Wiley said, "what have y'all been up to?"

Caroline piped up with a big grin, "Mil and I rode all the way to the top of the island today with John and Clyde. We saw some neat things along the way."

"We skied in the ocean, behind the Jeep, on the way back. That was really cool," Mil said.

Wiley smiled at the girls, then said, "That sounds like great fun. What are your plans tomorrow?"

"We are going home to get ready for camp. We hate to leave. We've had such a really good time," Mil said.

"That's right, I forgot. Your Aunt June told me that last week. Well, you can come back next summer as much as you want. That will be alright with you fellas, won't it?"

Clyde's eyes lit up as he said, "Yessir. You bet."

As the evening was wrapping up, Henry said, "Aunt Mildred, we'll be over tomorrow to take you and the girls to Harkers. We need to return Mr. Credle's skiff and pick up the Whirlwind too. When do you want to get away?"

"Thank you, Henry. I'd like to be on the road by noon, if that works for y'all."

"We'll be here about ten, to help you get loaded."

Mil and Caroline walked with John and Clyde, hand in hand to the Jeep. Little was said on our ride back to the A-Frame. They had no interest in talking about Wiley's war stories.

The next morning was more somber than if we had actually sunk the Whirlwind. It seemed that nothing Henry or I could say or do would pull our lovestruck companions from their funk.

During breakfast, Henry tried again. "Guys, did you hear us say there were *four* very cute girls on the beach yesterday? And that they all want to come out here when they're back next week?"

 "No, you didn't mention that, but I'm not very interested right now," Clyde said.

"OK, there's no hurry." But why don't we go ahead on over to the cottage now, to help the girls pack?" Henry said.

"Hey, that's a great idea. We don't have to wait until ten. Let's go," John shouted."

Clyde agreed by hopping up and charging out the back door. We were in the jeep moments later heading for the dock. After replacing our tanks with Mr. Credle's tanks, we were on our way.

The girls came out of the cottage waving enthusiastically when they saw our skiff. John gave it the gas and we raced ahead until we hit bottom a few yards from the shore. We sent John and Clyde ahead while we took care of the boat.

They hugged each other like they'd been parted for months and went inside. "That was a good idea Henry, you old softie."

"Nah. I was just sick of their whining."

"Um-hum."

Aunt Mildred added what looked like one of the last bags to the pile on the screen porch. "We'll start taking these to the boats. Will you be ready soon?" Henry asked.

"Yes, we are ready when you are."

Bags loaded, Clyde, John, Mil, and Caroline climbed into our skiff. Henry said, "Guess the rest of us will take this boat then."

Aunt Mildred smiled as Henry helped her aboard. I lifted Duna and Jane into the boat. Looking at her mom, Duna said, "Mom, this has been the best Cape trip ever."

"Best ever," Jane agreed.

"I'm glad girls," Mildred smiled. "I think your sisters enjoyed themselves too."

twenty

Preparing for the Storm

8:20 AM *Wednesday, August 27, 1969*

Sunlight beamed into the room as I sat in my bed wondering where the summer had gone. It had been a whirlwind of adventures, one after another. A tropical storm seemed a fitting end.

Slipping quietly out of bed, I grabbed a shirt and shorts and light-footed it down the steps to the kitchen. With the radio low, I listened for the latest information on the storm, while enjoying a bowl of cereal. After a few songs and commercials, the report came.

"Tropical storm Eve is off the coast of Jacksonville, Florida, traveling northeast at eleven miles-per-hour. Sustained winds are sixty miles-per-hour. The storm is expected to be off Cape Lookout tomorrow evening around nine o'clock. We will keep you posted."

Henry startled me when he pulled a stool up to the counter. John and Clyde followed.

"The storm's supposed to pass tomorrow night at nine, with winds over sixty," I said.

"That means great waves," Henry said.

"I was thinking the same thing. Unfortunately, we're supposed to be out of here tomorrow," I said.

"Yeah, I've gotta be at VES on Monday and there's no leeway," John said.

"Yeah, we start next week too," I said. "What if we clean and close up the houses today, surf tomorrow morning, and take off for Harkers after lunch?"

"That sounds good to me" John said, as Clyde and Henry nodded.

"All I've gotta do is close the shutters on my house. It's ready to go," Henry said."

"If we board up, clean, and pack up here," I suggested, "we can get some surfing in this afternoon. It's gotta be getting pretty good out there," I suggested.

"We can swing by Sally and Les's on the way back from Henry's to get some lunch and tell them goodbye," John said.

All agreed, we finished up breakfast and headed out to the shed for the plywood and hardware. It was a warm, sunny morning, with a light southerly breeze. A ribbon of white cumulonimbus clouds lined the ocean's southern horizon.

"Coast Guard's coming," Clyde said.

A large gray Dodge truck with a couple of guys, not much older than we were, pulled into the drive.

"Hey fellas," Clyde called out.

"Good morning," said the guy on the right, with a couple of stripes on his shirt. We're making sure everybody knows about the storm coming tomorrow night."

"We appreciate that," Clyde said. "We're closing up now and will leave tomorrow after some surfing."

"The waves should be impressive," the seaman said. Wish we could join you, but we'll be securing the boats. Y'all have a great time tomorrow. Keep a weather eye out. They can sneak up on you."

"Thanks fellas, we will," John waved as they pulled away.

John and Clyde went to work boarding and locking up the front windows. Walter had built a good system for protecting against storms and curious sightseers. Henry and I cleaned bathrooms and swept out the house. After an hour or so, we were busy closing Henry's house. Familiar with the shutters from the month before, we had closed and latched them by the time Henry was sure the gas and water were off, and the house was secure.

"Let's get some lunch," Henry shouted.

As we pulled out of the drive, I felt sad watching the house shrink in the distance behind us. The echoes of happy voices, shouts, and laughter played in my mind's ear. I wondered how John and Clyde were feeling as they thought of Mil and Caroline. They had grown summer-close during their two visits.

Les and Sally's back driveway was still. Around front we saw Les at the end of the dock, securing the davit for the wind.

"Can we help you with anything?" John yelled.

"No, everything's good."

Sally greeted us pleasantly as we filed into the store and took our seats at the counter.

"Are y'all staying tomorrow night?" Clyde asked, when Les walked in.

"We'll be here. This one doesn't look too bad," Sally said.

"Should stay mostly offshore, and the winds are manageable," Les added. "Isn't it about time you boys were headed back to school?"

"Yessir. We've boarded up and will head into Harkers tomorrow about lunchtime – after we ride some of those storm waves," Clyde said.

In a much more serious tone, Les said, "Boys, I trust your good judgement. Get to Harkers before the wind kicks up the Back Sound too badly. Watch out for each other in that ocean too. Riptides will be bad."

"Yessir, we will."

"Miss Sally, will you heat us up some lunch?" Henry asked.

"Surely will darlin'. We've got burgers, ham and cheeses, and meatloaf sandwiches," rummaging through the cellophane-wrapped sandwiches in the refrigerator.

"Can't eat ham," Henry said, "gives me nightmares." I'll have two hamburgers, please."

Clyde and I asked for burgers and John went for the meatloafs. Les headed into the back to continue his work.

"Get your drinks from the cooler boys." Sally said as she placed a couple of sandwiches into the Stewart oven and turned the dial for the infra-red light to begin doing its magic.

It would be the last hot meal of a great summer at Miss Sally's counter. When we were younger, Les would tell us the scariest ghost stories at the A-Frame. He and Sally watched us more closely and disciplined us when we needed it too. We hadn't needed it this summer, except maybe for the incident with Captain Bailey and the *Diamond City*. Our relationship was different. We were somewhere between ghost stories and adult-talk.

"I'm going to miss you both this winter," Clyde said. "Don't you two get lonely out here all by yourself?"

"That's mighty sweet Clyde. Livin' on this island is paradise for Les and me, with and without people. I think if we had to leave here, we'd just dry up. It was a real blessing when Charlie sold us this land so we could build our marina and home out here. It's the best place in the world for us."

Just then, a high-pitched tone came on the VHS radio followed by the words, "Sécurité, Sécurité, Sécurité." They preceded important Coast Guard warnings. After a few words, Sally turned it down to say, "Sounds like the storm continues moving like they thought. Don't wait too long tomorrow to get off."

"We won't," John said. "I'll sign that ticket for you."

Sally thanked him. "Here, you boys take the rest of these sandwiches for tonight and tomorrow."

Les came out from the back as we said goodbye for the season. Pulling away, I thought, with them here, we never really were without parents.

John headed for the beach road back to the A-Frame. Henry shouted, "Look at that surf. We gotta get back out there – now."

Following a quick turnaround to collect our boards from the shed, we headed back to the ocean to spend the rest of the day riding the building waves – already much better than usual.

It was near dusk when we packed it in. The A-Frame was dark and stuffy with the front boarded up.

"Too stuffy in here. Clyde, help me open a few of these portholes to get some breeze blowing," John snapped.

"Yessir Cap'n Ass." Clyde retorted. John just chuckled.

"It'll be worse in our bedroom. I'll open a few up there." I added.

Following a simple spaghetti dinner, we sat down at the poker table for cards. The radio played softly on the counter as lightning flashed in the southern portholes.

"Today was great, but tomorrow should be epic," Henry said.

"Yeah, but the last report said the storm's moving faster. Maybe we'd better leave before lunch," I said.

"Waa, waa," John cried mockingly. "The thing's not supposed to be here until eight-thirty tomorrow night. All we have to do is get in the boat and go."

"That's true butthead, but it could be blowing thirty or forty here by noon. Those kinds of winds will make some ugly waves on the Back Sound. Dad and Terry lost all these pilings in just a thunderstorm."

"Speaking of thunderstorms, this one's going to rain on us," Clyde said.

"You're right. Clyde and I'll get the bedroom. Y'all get these," I said.

Portholes sealed, Clyde said, "How 'bout a little poker guys?"

Dionne Warwick's "I'll Never Fall in Love Again" played on the radio as Clyde began handing out the chips and Henry shuffled the cards.

"Remember that time we skied through thunderstorm to see what that would be like?" Clyde asked. "The rain felt like needles in that wind."

"Yeah, the chopped-up water and lightening were different for sure," I laughed.

"But lots of fun." Clyde's voice got shriller as he continued. "The really cool part was that waterspout. Henry, it was about two feet thick and jumped around like a tail-walking swordfish – very hard to catch."

"Probably a good thing we didn't catch it," John chuckled.

"I have to agree there," Henry laughed.

After a few hands of cards, we called it a night. The bedroom was hot and stuffy, but the rain and wind on the roof helped sleep come quickly.

twenty one

Tropical Storm Eve

The bedroom was cold when I woke. Someone had opened the portholes when the rain stopped. Reaching for the covers I'd tossed aside the night before – it struck me how quiet it was outside. There were no crickets, gulls, or fishing boats. Was this the calm before the storm?

Pulling on shorts and a sweatshirt, I went downstairs for some breakfast and the latest on the storm. The Fifth Dimension was singing "Aquarius" when Clyde and Henry staggered down the steps.

Following the report, I said, "The surf could be better than we expected. Low tide was at six this morning. With a northeast wind, conditions look perfect. Clyde, pop some of these fresh batteries in the radio, so it won't die on us out there."

Batteries in, he cranked it up with "Pipeline" by the Ventures blaring.

"You're gonna' wake up John." I smiled.

"Hope so. It's time to get out there. Surf's calling dudes." Henry shouted.

Moments later, John stomped down the stairs. "You asses, I was sound asleep. What's the latest?" He asked, still groggy.

"Expected here, at eight-thirty tonight. Winds in the high 70's.

"How does the ocean look?

"Looked like a washing machine this morning from the third floor. That was low tide. It'll be getting better as the water comes in," I said.

A cool, stiff northeasterly breeze greeted us on the back deck. It would warm up as the sun rose. I tossed a canvas bag filled with sandwiches and water into the back of the Jeep as we walked by to get our boards.

With everyone on the Jeep, Henry shouted, "OK Eve, show us what you got."

Crossing the beach, we could hear the surf's roar over the engine. Our excitement grew as the salty mist dampened our faces and filled our nostrils.

When John rolled to a stop, Clyde shouted, "Let's try it here."

Moments later, we were in the suds, paddling out. The water felt warmer than the air and was charged with unusual energy.

Henry shouted, "These waves don't look like local boys."

"I know it." Clyde howled. "They're building into perfect 'A-Frames.' Gonna be awesome."

Clyde and Henry took off first. They were putting on a show. I tried a floater, sliding the board along the top of the wave sideways, with the fins out of the water. I came close to getting it right on the more powerful, perfectly shaped waves, but was still missing the technique, the skill or the practice needed. It didn't matter, we were having a blast.

On one of our party waves, Clyde shouted, "How much better can it get?"

Henry let out a howl and we all joined in.

After a couple of hours, I yelled to the group, "I'm heading in to check on the storm."

"Good idea," Henry shouted.

Gulping down some water, I flipped on the radio and heard the DJ say – "The latest on Tropical Storm Eve in five minutes. For you surfers out there here's a double play."

Following the Surfaris' "Wipe Out" and the Rivieras' "California Sun," the storm report suggested no change in track, time, or intensity.

I grabbed my board and headed back out to deliver the news. It was a struggle getting past the powerful breakers. "Guys, it's gusting in the high 30s. I think we should head back."

"Yeah, it's taking everything I've got to swim back out," Henry said.

We agreed to ride a couple more and head in.

Henry and Clyde let it all hang out. The waves curled high enough to shoot. One of my attempts rolled me all the way to the beach. Scuffed, scraped, and coughing up salty water with every breath, I was giddy with excitement. For one incredible moment, I surfed a pipeline – just before the longest, wildest wipeout I'd ever had. It was a blast – so hard to quit – so easy to quit.

The diagonal roll of the waves along the beach made for long, uninterrupted rides. I felt like the opening scene of the surfing movie *Endless Summer*. We stood tall for one last, long, unforgettable wave.

There was no carrying the boards once we got out of the water. We held them flat on the beach until John could block the wind with the Jeep. We sat on each one as we lifted them onto the bed. The driving sand stung as we made our way across the beach. Once beyond the runway and dunes, the wind and sand let up some. We could barely see the lighthouse through the haze of sand and salty mist. Visibility was no more than a quarter of a mile in any direction.

John backed the Jeep into the shed. We quickly unloaded the boards and secured the building for the storm. John and Henry boarded up the doors while Clyde and I went into the house for a final check. Clyde made sure that the front louvered windows were tightly closed and locked while I took a steel rod to ratchet down any portholes that hissed in the wind.

From the second floor, I tossed down our duffel bags and linens through the lattices. I was reminded of when, as kids, we had jumped from the third floor onto mattresses spread on the floor, twenty feet below. That we hadn't broken any bones was remarkable.

Clyde turned off the gas to the appliances while I emptied the refrigerator and freezer. I saved any food we might use on our ride home. Taking the trash and canvas bags to the back deck I saw that Henry and John were dropping the 2 x 6s across the shed vehicle doors.

Entering through the small, shed door, I got a shovel to bury the trash out back. Normally our degradable trash went to a landfill we managed about a mile from the house. We took glass bottles, jars, and anything else that wouldn't disintegrate to the mainland for recycling. But there was no time for this small amount of trash.

When I returned from the back, I shouted to the guys, "It's gusting 40's now. We'd better get out of here."

John nodded and slammed the shed door closed, making sure it locked. We grabbed our bags and walked under the house toward the sound, sticking close to the dunes for shelter against the strong easterly wind. There was so much sand swirling around, we walked with eyes closed, or down.

John yelled as loudly as he could, "I don't think Core Banks is going to block any of this wind."

"Oh really, ya think?" I yelled back, feeling vindicated.

We brushed and bumped into each other repeatedly as the powerful gusts knocked us about. When we got to the dock, the Whirlwind looked like she'd been abandoned to the elements, with her windward lines stretched like piano strings.

Clyde was first to the dock. When he jumped up, the wind nearly flattened him. He had to get down on all-fours to crawl down the dock. We did the same.

Throwing our bags into the boat, we jumped aboard and secured loose items for the rough, wet ride to Harkers. Clyde pumped the bulb on the fuel line to charge the engine, while Henry and I cleared the downwind dock lines.

Clyde yelled to John, "OK, fire her up."

The motor just spun and spun until Clyde yelled, "Hold on John, you'll run the battery down.

Clyde unclamped the engine cover. When he lifted it, I grabbed him to keep them both from blowing overboard. I helped lower the cover into the boat and he immediately went to work checking the engine. He started with the fuel line to make sure the engine was getting gas. Then he followed the electrical wires from the battery into the engine, looking for any breaks or loose connections. He ran his fingers along the red wire coming into the motor, then to the ignition coil. He pulled the top off the coil, exposing the terminals. Crossing the points that feed the spark plugs with a screwdriver, he yelled to John, "OK, give it a spin."

Same as before, the motor just spun until Clyde motioned John to stop.

"This coil's dead! There's no fire getting to the spark plugs."

Clyde's words were final. An outboard motor without a working coil is dead. We all knew it.

"Looks like we've got a date with Eve on the Cape tonight," Henry screamed.

"We can't leave the boat tied like this. It'll swamp." John yelled. "Anchoring out won't work either. The bilge pump's still full of splinters. We'd better pull her up on the beach and throw a couple of anchors out. I'll go back and get the Jeep."

"I'll go with you," Clyde shouted.

"We'll get the lines and anchors ready."

We replaced the engine cover and went about readying the boat for pull-out. The stinging sand and wind made everything difficult.

Minutes later, Clyde and John appeared from the dusty mist in the Jeep.

"Henry, look, the Martians have landed," I shouted.

"Hah! Now that's thinking."

Clyde and John were wearing scuba masks. Their tee shirts were tucked under the nose piece to protect their faces, mouths, and lungs from the blasting sand.

"Hope they brought extras!"

"Me too."

John drove around the end of the dock and quickly backed down between the dunes. Clyde hopped out and handed us some goggles. After pulling them on, we gave him hearty pats on the back. The improvement was amazing. We could see considerably further and without pain.

After securing the long line from the boat to the Jeep, Henry, Clyde, and I made our way back down the dock to the boat. We released the downwind lines and gave John the signal to slowly pull the boat's bow toward the beach.

Once we were far enough from the dock, we released the windward stern line and the boat quickly swung into the wind. With the bow facing the shore, John floored the Jeep to gain as much momentum as he could. We three moved to the stern to lift the bow so the boat could be pulled as far ashore as possible. Our feet felt the vibration of sand on the bottom, just before the boat suddenly stopped. We jumped out and pushed for a couple more feet.

Anchors set and gear transferred, we climbed aboard the Jeep, and laughed at each other's appearance. But even with the improvement, the blowing sand and mist had reduced visibility to no more than fifty yards in any direction. We drove slowly along the beach for what seemed an unusually long time until the gray-white roof of the A-Frame suddenly appeared over us. It looked like a giant spaceship, with layers of black eyeballs watching our return.

John shoved the floor shifter into 4-wheel drive and blasted over the dune. The driveway, encircled by the shed, dunes, and house, offered some relief from the wind.

Clyde, Henry, and I jumped out to open the shed for John. It was a welcome relief to be inside, out of the sand and wind. However, most of the wind noise remained, making conversation difficult.

"I'll turn on the propane." John shouted. "We won't need the generator – the water tanks are full."

Looking around for anything we might need, before closing up, I grabbed a couple of large nine-volt flashlights off the workbench. With masks pulled back down over our eyes, we grabbed our duffels and prepared for the walk across the drive to the A-Frame.

The wind seemed to be blowing a lot harder. We walked in a tight group, holding our bags in one hand and the closest person with the other. We were still bounced around.

John was at the back door first. We huddled around him to block the wind as he turned the knob. The door blew open violently, almost taking his hand with it. We squeezed through the narrow passage, one-by-one, with our bags of supplies in hand. It took all four of us to push the door closed and three to hold it while John dropped the 2x6 across the two doors.

The house was dark, and still. The wind screamed like banshees outside, but the house was much quieter than the shed had been. I made my way over to the stove with the flashlight and lit a match. It was amazing that the flame hardly flickered, with wind blowing forty miles-an-hour just inches on the other side of the wall.

"We've got to get some air in here," Clyde blurted out. "Until it starts raining, let's open a couple of portholes on the lee side."

"Good idea," John agreed.

Henry and I unloaded the food bag onto the counter while John relit the pilots for the refrigerator and the hot water heater.

"We've got spaghetti, C-Rations, ham and cheese, PB&J, Vienna sausages, Chips Ahoy, and cereal," I said.

Clyde reached for a spaghetti kit and said, "I love the cinnamon buns that come in these packs."

"I don't know about your food choices Clyde," Henry said as he pulled over a can of Vienna sausages.

"I'm sticking with the winning side. As I recall Henry, the U.S. Army whipped those Vienna boys."

"You've got a point," Henry said, pulling the top off and beginning the challenge of getting the first sausage out of the can.

John and I picked up ham and cheese sandwiches. "Jumping Jack Flash" by The Rolling Stones played as we wrapped up our late lunch and moved to the game table for some cards.

The intensity of lightening and thunder increased steadily through the afternoon. The air became musty again, as we'd closed the portholes hours earlier, when the rain started falling in buckets. The A-Frame was rocking in the heavy gusts. The radio news had said that local winds were in the mid-sixties and two tornadoes had landed Down East.

"Well folks, I hope you're safely sheltered now. Here's a song to slow things down a bit, by Jay and the Americans, called "Hushabye.""

We had to raise our voices by half to be heard over the wind, rain, and thunder.

"I'm going to get something to eat," Henry said. We joined him around the kitchen counter to pick over the remaining sandwiches, cookies, and Army rations for dinner.

"Maybe I'll try one of these U.S. Army C-Rations." Henry opened the box and poured out a can of spaghetti, peaches, cinnamon roll, a three-pack of Marlboro cigarettes, and a small Hershey bar. "Wow, there're a lot of goodies in here."

"See, I told you so," Clyde gloated. "Please don't smoke though."

We were soon around the table again, nibbling on the last of our hockey-puck-shaped cinnamon buns. Clyde opened a pack of Chips Ahoy as I shuffled the cards.

"Turn up the radio," John asked. "Can't hear it over the racket."

Donovan was singing "Atlantis."

"Great, now they're playing songs about sinking cities," Henry said.

Dealing the cards, I said, "Let's play a game of Spades."

"I wonder if the floor'll get wet tonight?" Clyde asked.

"It would take a lot more wind than this to blow in the ten feet needed to reach this floor. This one's a baby," John said.

"Well, she's a noisy baby," Henry said.

"You know, this kinda reminds me of those rainy sleepover nights we had in the back yard in Dad's camper," Clyde said.

"Yeah, the wet canvas and wood smelled kinda like it does in here," I said.

"It was fun watching those old sci-fi movies on your dad's portable TV," John added. That screen couldn't have been more than four inches square."

"Yeah, it was small, but crystal clear, especially those two UHF channels" Clyde said.

"I loved Japanese monster movies like Godzilla and King Kong," Henry said. "Watching the buildings curl up like paper when they burned with those big flames was hilarious. The way they mouthed about ten words to say 'OK' or 'look out' was hilarious."

"How about those movies with mad scientists? I said. We have a crazy scientist at the table. A couple of years ago Clyde got a chemistry set for Christmas. He got real excited when he learned he could make explosive compounds. After a week of grinding and mixing, he had a pile of gunpowder that was a foot tall. He decided to test it one night. The same night our parents were preparing for a dinner party." The pounding wind and thunder outside added suspense to my story.

"Clyde pulled aside a small amount to test. When he struck his match, *snap!* . . . The match head took off on its own, toward the ceiling, then down, straight for the middle of Clyde's huge pile of gunpowder. He jumped up as sparks began to fly. A loud roar started as flames shot up like a rocket, then down toward the floor. The fire was so bright, I was sure I saw Clyde's skeleton.

"When the flame died down and the entire house was black with smoke, a blood-curdling scream, more terrifying than any sci-fi movie, came from downstairs. 'Clyde Bass, I'm going to *kill you.*'

"We got to the top of the stairs just in time to see Dad step in front of our pan-wielding mother. He wrapped her into a bear hug and just held her. Seconds later, Bill Lawrence's voice boomed from the side door – 'Mary Carolyn, have you been cooking again?' Clyde's life was saved, and we were a family again, just in time to tell the fire department the house wasn't on fire.

"Well done, Clyde," Henry said, chuckling. "You're as crazy as I am."

"I've been meaning to ask you about that Henry." Clyde said. "Why *are* you so crazy?"

Henry chuckled. Then his face fell and his eyes dulled. "I had an older brother, named Wiley, after my father. Wiley wanted to be wild, like the stories he'd heard my dad and uncle tell of their boyhoods. He hung out with older boys because they were wild like he wanted to be.

"One summer afternoon he and his friends were riding bikes on a narrow country road. Wiley took a quick turn without looking and was run over."

"Henry, that's awful. I'm sorry," Clyde said.

Nodding in appreciation, he continued. "You all know my little brother Richard, from summers out here. You remember how awkward he was around people. He got teased so badly at home that my parents sent him off to school in Asheville this past year. They teased him mercilessly there too. He ran off all his roommates and was living alone by the end of the semester. This past Christmas he told my parents he didn't want to go back there. Daddy said he needed to finish the year he'd started. Well, he finished it alright – with a double barrel shotgun behind the shed out back. It was days before they found him."

Clyde, John, and I were speechless. *There was the look of deep sadness I'd seen in my friend's eyes so many times before.*

"They later found a note saying he blamed girls for shunning him and that he just didn't fit in . . ."

I guess with both my brothers dead, and the possibility of going to Vietnam, nothing much mattered anymore. Guess I went kind of crazy. Didn't give a damn."

Over the thunder and wind, Clyde spoke up. "I'm really sorry Henry. I know how Richard felt. Kids laugh at me because I read and write slow. I see letters and numbers different than everybody else.

"Mom and Dad sent me to military school when I started fighting and acting up. It was the worst time of my life. If our guns weren't fake, I might have shot myself too. I don't know. It's not Mom and Dad's fault, they were just trying to help me. It's my fault for being stupid."

"You are *not* stupid Clyde!" John said, with surprising tenderness. "Do you remember that twelve horsepower motor you found on the side of the road? You said you could double your go cart's power with it."

Clyde nodded, with a faint twinkle.

"You had it in a hundred parts on the garage floor when your mom said you dad was coming home in an hour and wanted to park in the garage. I've never seen anybody work faster or smarter than you did putting that motor together. When your mom called us up for dinner, you gave that engine a pull, and the thing started up like new."

Clyde nodded, fighting back a smile, and said, "I love working on motors. Motor parts don't ever look backwards to me. I'm just not cut out for reading and writing."

"And that's OK. You're great with machines and you're even better with people," I said. "People get a kick out of beating around you. The guys who make fun of you are jealous.

"I know school's hard, and I'm not making light. You may see words and numbers differently, but that doesn't make you stupid. You remember everything you hear. Mom says the doctors tell her you learn differently than they teach in public school. They are doing the best they can to find a place that's right for you."

"Clyde," Henry joined in. "I'm real glad your guns at military school weren't real. Just wouldn't be the same around here without you." He said smiling.

Looking him in the eye, Clyde said, "Thank you Henry. I'm sorry about Richard."

"I am too," Henry said, putting a hand on Clyde's shoulder.

"Guys," I said, "I've got something I want to say. Henry, when you said that girls shamed Richard, I know the feeling. Maybe not to the level of hurt he must have felt, but it still hurts. For the last couple of years, I've felt left behind in high school. A lot of the kids I grew up with have moved easily into the social and academic requirements of high school. I feel left behind and pushed out. I didn't make the football team. Didn't get asked to join any civic clubs. And didn't get into all the advanced academic classes I wanted.

"I like it out here because I'm myself around you guys and feel like one of the guys. I'm good at the things we do and love the crazy fun we have doing them.

"You know Henry, it was good being with you that afternoon at Atlantic Beach when you walked up to those four girls, just as cool as you please. Within a minute, you had us sitting with them. We carried on like old friends – no, not like old friends – like exciting *new* friends. Those girls were just as excited to be with *me* as I was with *them*."

"That was a fun afternoon. I think what's-her-name really liked you," Henry said.

"Yeah Lisa, thanks." I smiled.

"I'll tell you something, Henry continued with both hands on the table. "My time our here with you guys, doing all the crazy stuff we've done, has been good for me – painful sometimes – but good. I did some really bad drugs at VES, and the first couple of weeks here. But I stopped. The crazy things we've done, have given me a better way to work out all my mess."

"That's great Henry. You still do crazy stuff, but you've dialed it back," I said.

Just then, the radio announcer came on, "We interrupt this broadcast to bring you a special bulletin from the National Hurricane Center. Tropical Storm Eve is off the coast of Cape Lookout, NC. Sustained winds are currently seventy-five miles-per-hour with gusts up to eighty. The storm surge is expected to be three to four feet. Residents in low-lying areas are advised to stay off the roads. Now back to our regular programming."

Minutes later, the plywood sheets on the front of the house began rattling and banging so fiercely we were concerned they'd break the windows.

"Guys, I think we'd be safer in our bedroom in case any of this glass breaks," John said.

We all agreed and took some cards and food up. Over the next couple of hours, the winds slowed. By about three in the morning, the rains stopped, so we could open the portholes and let in the amazingly fresh air. Wearied from the long day, sleep came quickly. My last thoughts were a prayer of thanks for getting through the storm and for the truths we'd learned from each other, on the eve of manhood.

twenty two

Going Home

We were up at first light, eager to get to Sally and Les's for them to radio and let our parents know we were OK. The morning air was crisp and the sky clear blue. Lots of standing water remained on the island, but we were able to get around it by running along dunes when required.

"It's always beautiful after tropical storms and hurricanes. They're like giant vacuum cleaners," I said.

"Glad this one didn't suck us up," Clyde joked. "Hope the Whirlwind made it through."

"Yeah, we'll go to the dock after making our radio call and checking on Henry's house," John said.

With the runway under a foot of water, John crossed over to the beach. The cuts and ridges left by the draining surge water and pounding surf made progress slow.

When we pulled into their driveway, Les came out of his shed to greet us. "Didn't expect to see you boys. Everything OK?"

"Couldn't get the Whirlwind started yesterday," I said. "We spent the night. Can you call Mr. Credle and ask him to let our parents know we're OK?

Les turned immediately and led us inside to his radio. Mr. Credle answered the hail the first try and said he would call the Reeves, Bass, and Long families at once. After the call, Les said he kept a spare outboard coil in reserve and was sure it would work on our motor. He would meet us at the boat later that morning to help us get it installed.

Les said there was too much standing water around Henry's house to get there by Jeep and it looked alright in the binoculars. Les said he would check it later, when the water went down.

We headed out, saying goodbye to Sally and telling Les we'd be at the boat in a couple of hours, packed and ready to go. It took about half that time to get back to the dock. After several u-turns, re-routes, and John's fading patience, we were thrilled to find that the Whirlwind had survived. Enough storm water remained under her to push her off the shore and over to the dock for tie up.

After another hour, we had the A-Frame cleaned, closed down, and locked. Our walk to the boat from the house was a wet one. There were numerous one and two-foot pools of water along the sound's shoreline. Carrying bags in both hands, it wasn't possible to keep them out of the water.

"Looks like the Cape's being as difficult on our leaving as she was when we first got here," I said.

"I think she's doing all she can to keep us here," Clyde said. "And I kinda like that."

Finally, at the boat, we began stowing our gear when Clyde said, "Hey, there's Les. He's coming by boat."

"Les knows how to get around the Cape today," Henry observed.

Les tied just a bow line to the dock and hopped from his boat into ours with a small bag of tools and the part. I brought Les up to speed on our near sinking while he and Clyde worked. By the time the story was finished, the new coil was installed.

"Give her a spin John. Let's see what we've got." Les said in his calm voice.

The motor fired up as quickly and loudly as usual. We shouted and pumped fists into the air as Les coolly gathered his tools and climbed into his boat. We wanted to hug him, but Les wasn't the hugging kind. We said our thankyous and goodbyes and saw him off. As he motored away, I marveled at how much he embodied the same spiritual, tranquility of the Cape. They really were inseparable.

The trip back to Harkers was a quiet one. We were all more than a little crestfallen that our crazy, fun-filled adventures were in our wake – until next summer anyway.

We made quick work of unloading the boat and packing our cars at the marina. We went in together to say goodbye to Mr. Credle. He said that our parents didn't sound too worried about us through the storm, confident in our decisions. I wondered how much he had varnished that report, but I loved that man for his varnish. We each hugged him long and firmly and said our farewells for the season. Walking out, we promised to come back as soon as we could.

By the cars, we hugged Henry and wished him a better year at VES.

"I'm not going back to VES. I'm going to finish high school at home, in Roanoke Rapids."

"Wow, that's a surprise Henry. When were you going to tell me?" John asked, sounding hurt.

"It's a recent decision. I talked about it with my mom when she was here in July and let them know of my decision a couple of weeks ago. They were happy with it."

"Wow Henry, that's good to hear. Sounds like you're happy too," Clyde said.

"Yeah, I'm glad to be going home."

We said goodbye and hopped into the Mustang and Henry into his '62 Carolina Blue Ford Econoline, which was so Henry.

The three of us were quiet and reflective at first, as we wound our way along the curvy Down East roads. But, by Havelock, we were reliving our summer adventures. Clyde reminded John how he'd saved him from Cynthia at Mrs. Willis' fruit stand. They came alive as they reminisced about their times with Caroline and Mil.

Recalling our near sinking, I told the guys that I was going to pay for the damage with earnings from my upcoming job at Lazarus' Drug Store. Dad had appreciated that and said he would talk to Uncle Charlie about it.

Pulling into the farm drive, John said, "I have got a ton of stuff to do this weekend to get ready for school."

We stopped at the tennis court to say hello to Uncle Charlie and Lindy Mace, who looked to be having a pretty heated match. Charlie said, "Good to have you boys home safely. John, I'm going to fly you up to VES on Sunday."

"Thanks Dad. It's good to be home," John said.

At the house, Aunt Sarah came out to greet us as we started pulling bags from the car. She assured John that she had him mostly ready for school. Only the extras he wanted to take needed his attention. Clyde and I wished him a good semester at school and hugged Aunt Sarah goodbye.

Windows down, the smell of fresh-cut pasture grass wafted through the car in the soft afternoon light of early fall. It smelled like home. It was good to be back.

On the way through town, I decided to swing by the tennis courts and pool. There wouldn't be anybody there this time of day, but I was curious if I might feel more confident in that place. What was this new school year going to be like? I'd definitely be a better friend to the friends I had. And I'd be bolder in making new ones. I'd been successfully bold with Tracy and the four girls on Atlantic Beach. Yes, there *was* a new Sam in town – home from the Edge.

"Why are you smiling Sam?" Clyde asked.

"Oh . . . just thinking about the new school year. I'm gonna make some changes."

"I know you'll do great. I wish I could."

Don't think like that. Remember our talk last night? You've got a lot going for you. Start with that."

A warmth washed over me as we pulled into our driveway. Sister Emily hopped off the trampoline and ran over to give us hugs. Mom ran from the side porch arms up. Dad was due home from the office soon.

Dinner was earlier than usual. Mom had prepared fried chicken, corn, green beans, and rolls. That was unique because Mom was more of a TV dinner, macaroni and cheese, chicken pot pie sort of cook. She proudly boasted coming from a long line of non-cooks.

After the blessing, as we passed the serving dishes around, Dad said, "Kids, your mom and I have some exciting news to share.

Clyde, Emily, and I stopped passing, eager to hear the coming announcement.

"As you know," Dad continued. "Clyde has had a difficult time in school these last few years. Your mom and I have talked to lots of experts, but their recommendations are inconsistent. So, your mother and I have decided," looking directly at Clyde, "that you will do better going to high school in Morehead City. West Carteret has strong machine and metal working programs, which are right up your ally."

Clyde's face lit up. Emily's and mine were more puzzled.

"I've rented an apartment in Morehead City and gotten you enrolled at West Carteret High for the upcoming semester. Mom and I bought a lot in Mansfield Park and plan to build a house there. We will be together as a family as much as possible, in Sanford for the holidays, and Morehead for the summers. The house should be ready by next summer."

"I can't believe this!" Clyde said, looking and sounding more like he was returning home than leaving it.

"Mom, Dad, I think this is a great idea. Clyde and I were just talking about how much he loves Morehead. I'm completely for it."

"What about our family? We'll be split up." Emily asked with a quivering voice.

Gently placing her hand on Emily's shoulder, Mom said, "This has not been an easy decision, but your father and I feel strongly that we need to be together as a family in this decision. Do you think we can do this for Clyde?"

"Yes mam, I know we can," Emily said, sounding far more mature than her thirteen years.

It was decided.

After dinner, we settled into the den to watch *Get Smart, He and She, and Hogans Heroes*. When the CBS Friday Night Movie came on, Clyde and I went upstairs at Emily's bedtime, exhausted from our long day and eager to sleep in our own beds.

Turning off the wagon-wheel lamp between our beds, Clyde said, "I can't believe my family would do this for me. I'm so excited and so relieved I don't have to go back to Central."

"It's going to be a lot different around here without you and Dad. A lot duller for sure. You know, I get the feeling Dad could use a break from Sanford too. Ever since selling his business, he's been trying lots of new things – like painting, photography, and music. He and Uncle Charlie seem to argue more these days too. Morehead might be the best thing for both of you."

"Yeah, I've noticed that too," Clyde said. But moving to a new town and school is scary."

"Scarier than surfing storm waves, or a car hood at fifty miles an hour, jumping over a four-foot ski rope, or keeping a boat from sinking across six miles of open water? And Caroline – you seemed very comfortable around her.

"You and Dad are great at meeting new people and taking on new challenges. You'll make Morehead home quickly. I admire you both and plan to spend my year trying new things and meeting new people to make Central feel like home for me.

"You admire me?" Clyde asked, with a quiver in his voice.

"More than anybody." You're the bravest, craziest, most fun-loving person I know. You, little brother, are my hero."

The room was quiet. I closed my eyes and thanked God for the moment, for my family, for the adults who were always there for me, and for my brothers-of-the-summer. We danced along the edges until we found our way back home.

Acknowledgements

A memoir is a solitary journey, supported by memories of family and friends who lived the story with me. I've taken great care to be sensitive to their feelings and not to create too great a wake through the tranquil pool of family life and friendship.

There's no question that my brother Clyde is the hero of this book. I wish he was here to share in it. I am blessed by the life we had together and for the contributions he made to this memoir.

Thanks also to the other two supporting leads. My dear friend Henry Long provided numerous *no way* moments and openly shared a painful time in his life. Cousin John was as close as a brother growing up. Without him, there would not have been any farm years *or* Cape years. I can't imagine how different my life would be, for better or worse, had I not benefitted from the transformative benefits of risk, and adversity they offered.

Thanks also to my cousins, Terry, David, and Suzanne Reeves. Their legendary adventures, proceeding ours by a few years, left huge roles for us to fill. Their tales could fill volumes if pressed onto pages. Thank you for sharing the amazing accomplishments of your parents, Charlie, and Sarah through all the stories, photographs, letters, and documents. Their vision for and stewardship of the Cape during the years leading up to the Cape Lookout National Seashore are material for a much more graceful story than much of what was written in newspaper and magazine articles of the day.

Thank you, Mary Frances Credle Wright, Bud Doughton, and Mason Williams, for your stories and color added to this book.

As this is my first book, a certain amount of urging and prodding was required. The story was conceived more than a decade ago as a novel. Thank you, Sharon Bass, for keeping the spark alive through your encouragement and example. Her paintings inspire.

By the spring of 2022, I was writing in earnest, but it seemed, in the wrong direction. Special thanks to gifted writer and coach, Emily Carter, for walking with me through the change to memoir. She gets most of the credit for the title too. And thank you for introducing me to author Chris Laney. Chris' guidance through the intimidating world of self-publishing has been invaluable.

I want to thank my gifted, patient, and excellent editor Jan Parker. The initial stages felt like surgery without anesthesia, but her direct, yet graceful tutelage quickly became collaborative, for which I am forever grateful. Thanks also, to my wonderful second editor, and first wife Jane Langley Brothers. She knows so many of these stories firsthand.

Beta readers are indispensable friends to any author – the kinds of friends who share their honest critiques, confident the friendship will withstand them. I am blessed to have had a large group of readers willing to share their time and wisdom in this endeavor. I am deeply grateful to my sister, Emily Baumgartner, author Emily Carter, Cousin John Reeves, and avid readers Laurel Wilkerson, Sheila Flanagan, Bruce Berger, Susan Elliott, Daughter Langley Cumbie, Daughter Emily Shepard, and Jane Langley Brothers. Thank you all for enduring a very rough first draft.

Equally important has been the unvarnished feedback of four creative authors in our reading critique group, *Story Swappers*. Emily Carter, Autumn Ware, Melissa Kelly, and Jesi Waugh. You have spent hours coaching me to be a better writer and helping to make "Boys on the Edge" as good as it can be. Thank you.

I've been blessed to have a small village of dear friends in support of this project.

About the author

Sam was born in Beaumont, Texas, and raised in Sanford, North Carolina. He received a B.A. from Hampden-Sydney College in Virginia and an M.B.A. from Wake Forest University. After more than forty years in wealth management, during which he wrote hundreds of "Friday Briefs" to his clients, he now enjoys writing full time in his home on the Outer Banks of North Carolina. He is currently working on an artificial intelligence thriller novel he hopes to publish early next year.

Notes

[1] Steppenwolf's "Born to Be Wild" 1968
https://music.apple.com/us/album/born-to-be-wild/1440859623?i=1440860171

[2] The Shocking Blue – "Venus" 1969
https://music.apple.com/us/album/venus/293336477?i=293336485

[3] The Vogues – "Hawaii Five-O" 1969
https://music.apple.com/us/album/hawaii-five-o/716663683?i=716663766

[4] The Doors – "Hello I Love You" 1968
https://music.apple.com/us/album/hello-i-love-you/640047463?i=640047755

[5] The Younbloods – "Get Together" 1969
https://music.apple.com/us/album/the-best-of-the-youngbloods/299558073

[6] Jr Walker & the All Stars – "What Does It Take to Win Your Love" 1969
https://music.apple.com/us/album/
what-does-it-take-to-win-your-love/1635873264?i=1635873270

[7] Strawberry Alarm Clock – "Incense and Peppermint" 1969
https://music.apple.com/us/album/incense-and-peppermint/1452852926?i=1452852935

[8] Every Mother's Son – "Come on Down to My Boat Baby" 1969
https://music.apple.com/library/playlist/p.AWXopqlTLNkmpa

[9] Dusty Springfield – "I Only Want to Be with You." 1963
https://music.apple.com/us/album/i-only-want-to-be-with-you/1436881148?i=1436881516

[10] The Cape Hatteras light is painted with black stripes resembling a barber pole. The Cape Lookout lighthouse is built with the same design but is painted with large black and white diamonds. It is said that the original paint crews reversed the paint schemes. The Hatteras light was supposed to get the diamonds to mark Diamond Shoals, just off her coast. Locals believe the painters knew better than Washington. There had been a maritime village on Shackleford Banks back in the 1800's, not far from Cape Lookout, called Diamond City. The villagers processed whale blubber into oil. They also made tar from the sap of local pine trees. When mixed with hemp thread, it was pounded between the wooden planks on ships to make them watertight.

The village was destroyed in 1899 by a hurricane. The horses they used to haul their wagons and sleds were left behind. Their offspring remain there, on Shackleford and Carrot Islands, across from

Beaufort. Another legend suggests the horses swam ashore from sinking Spanish ships in the early 1700's."

The ocean between Cape Lookout and Cape Hatteras is known as the 'Graveyard of the Atlantic.' More than 5,000 ships have gone down out there since they started keeping records in the early 1500's. They were forced to navigate the rough and narrow straits out there as they sailed southward to the Spanish colonies in Florida and the Caribbean

The Gulf Stream is a wide, powerful sea current of warm water that flows north from the Gulf of Mexico. It is squeezed close to our coastline because it reaches so far into the Atlantic. Ships traveling south have to get very close to the dangerous shoals of Hatteras and Lookout to avoid the north-moving current. It didn't take much for storms or decoy fires, intentionally set by pirates, to run them aground.

[11] The Friends of Distinction – "Grazing in the Grass" 1969
https://music.apple.com/us/album/grazing-in-the-grass/305781875?i=305781884

[12] The Who – "I Can See for Miles" 1969
https://music.apple.com/us/album/i-can-see-for-iles/1440743116?i=1440743127

[13] Paul Mauriat – "Love is Blue" 1969
https://music.apple.com/us/album/love-is-blue/1400662348?i=1400662356

[14] The Fifth Dimension – "Aquarius" 1969
https://music.apple.com/us/album/one-less-bell-to-answer/298386984?i=298387476

[15] The story as more completely told by Dr. Graham Barden III. "A couple of hurricanes in '32 and '33 opened up a small channel from Back Sound into the Cape Lookout Bight and ocean. It was a blessing because it gave Harkers fishermen quick access to the ocean. Before the channel, they had to row fifteen miles to the Beaufort Inlet to get out. My friend David Yoemans said, 'It wasn't so bad going out as it was coming back, when you was haulin' ten thousand pounds of fish.'

"By 1934, the channel filled back in and Harkers fishermen were once again forced to row to Beaufort to get out to the fishing grounds.

My granddad was elected to the U.S. Congress that year. As a junior congressman, he was put on a few piddly committees, but he took great interest in one of them – the House Committee on Rivers and Harbors. It controlled the dredging of waterways.

"My granddad's first act in Congress was to get his committee to add the channel to the "Must Dredge List" for the Army Corps of Engineers. Soon after, the Corps opened up a thirty-foot wide channel through the sand to create what is now known as Barden's Inlet.

"The people of Harkers were so excited about the new channel that they wanted to put up a statue of my father. Some even named babies after him."

[16] Story as told by Dr. Graham Barden III of his father. "As a boy, my dad loved the Cape just as much we did. He had a little 16-foot flat-bottomed skiff with a three horsepower Briggs & Stratton engine. He'd drive that little boat all the way from New Bern to Miss Carry's store, which sat right out there, in our front yard. Took the better part of a day at eight miles-an-hour.

"Years later, when Dad and Mom Mary got married, Sam Whitehurst, my dad's law partner, gave them a lot on the Cape as a wedding present. He'd gotten it from a client he'd did some legal work for out here."

"In 1957, Dad learned the Coast Guard was accepting bids to move or destroy the chief lighthouse keeper's quarters. I beat the other bidder and hired Jimmy Collins from New Bern to move the house. He did it with a bulldozer and a lo-boy trailer."

"The local fishermen took bets on just that possibility, Clyde. I don't know how he did it either, but ole Jimmy was a resourceful guy.

"The power lines connecting the lighthouse to the Coast Guard station blocked him from moving yet house. When Jimmy asked permission to drop them temporarily, the Chief told him he'd have to get permission from Washington. Jimmy was to check back that afternoon. Well, Jimmy returned to his job, cut the lines, drove the house over them, and spliced them back, good as new.

"Later that afternoon as the house was being lowered onto its new foundation here, Jimmy returned to the Coast Guard station, as he'd promised. The chief apologized saying that his request to disturb government property had been denied.

"Jimmy said 'Chief, I'm sorry, but I've already moved the house.' Pointing out the window, he said, 'She's settling onto her new foundation right now. I was so sure the government wouldn't mind if we dropped the lines to get that house off their property—like they wanted—I went ahead and cut the line and reconnected it. Do you think they want me to put the house back?'"

[17] Kenny Rogers – "Ruby Don't Take Your Love to Town" 1969
https://music.apple.com/us/album/
ruby-dont-take-your-love-to-town/1496051826?i=1496052117

[18] Puffing on his cigar, Charlie said, "Well, a Canadian partner named Brian Newkirk and I started buying land in 1953 with the purpose of developing a unique beach resort. In 1955, we bought a large tract from Judge Luther Hamilton, but were stalled with the unexpected death of Newkirk, and delays in settling his estate.

"Five years later, O.T. Sloan joined me to buy Newkirk's 50% interest from his estate. He pointed southward, "That's when we sold Les and Sally three acres to build their marina and home. We planned to build a subdivision close by. Two years later, Sam and Mary Carolyn bought O.T.'s interest and the development became a family project."

"What was the state doing during this time?" Bill Lawrence asked.

Senator Staton answered. "In the late 50s and early 60s, they were concerned that storm erosion of the Outer Banks from hurricanes Hazel and Donna would expose the coastal mainland directly to the forces of the Atlantic Ocean. The General Assembly passed an appropriation bill that allowed the state to purchase certain properties on the Outer Banks to build up the Banks."[18]

"We've always assumed," Charlie added "based on our conversations with Governors Sanford and Moore, that Cape Lookout extended so far from the mainland that it offered no practical coastal protection. Based on several such conversations, we thought we'd be free to continue with our development plans, without interference.

"But since then, we've been slow walked by the State and the Carteret Planning Commission on every permit we've requested. We've learned that five years ago, the State Property Officer asked the Commission to withhold approval of our sub-division since the state was going to buy our land for the purpose of turning it over to the Federal Government for a national park. In all that time, we've not been approached once by the state. They've blocked our efforts to use the land as we intended when we bought it and they've made no offer to buy it. They've frozen property values for their convenience, at our expense. It's an invasion of individual property rights."

[19] Dad said, "It was quite a feat building a structure like the A-Frame on this remote sandbar. From the very start we had challenges and more than a few catastrophes. Charlie and I drew his inspiration for this structure on a napkin when we were having lunch one day. The foundation and structure consist of twenty, fifty-foot power poles. Due to their length and weight, Terry and I decided to drag them out here with the Whirlwind. Unfortunately, a pop-up thunderstorm hit us hard in the middle of the sound. Waves broke some of the cables that held them together. They were scattered all over the sound. It took us days to locate and gather the strays.

"Sinking them in perfect position was Tommy Eure's job. He and his men jetted the poles twelve to fifteen feet into the sand in pairs forming 'A's. They winched each pair together with come-alongs and bound them with stainless steel cables. Ten pairs were placed in a row to form this structure."

Joists were bolted between the pilings to form the three floors. When finished, the crew joked that they had built a three-story dock."

[20] David Bowie – "Space Oddity" 1969
https://music.apple.com/us/album/space-oddity/697650603?i=697651126

[21] "Hello, Neil and Buzz. I'm talking to you by telephone from the Oval Room at the White House. And this certainly has to be the most historic telephone call ever made. I just can't tell you how proud we all are of what you've done. For every American, this has to be the proudest day of our lives. And for people all over the world, I am sure they too join with Americans in recognizing what an immense feat this is. Because of what you have done, the heavens have become a part of man's world. And as you talk to us from the Sea of Tranquility, it inspires us to redouble our efforts to

bring peace and tranquility to Earth. For one priceless moment in the whole history of man, all the people on this Earth are truly one: one in their pride in what you have done, and one in our prayers that you will return safely to Earth." Shortly before midnight, July 20, 1969, Richard M. Nixon spoke from the Oval Office to astronauts Neil Armstrong and Edwin Aldrin in the Sea of Tranquility, on the Moon

[22] L.E.M. Lunar Excursion Module – the vehicle that landed on the moon. The top portion of the vehicle blasted off from the surface of the moon to return astronauts Neil Armstrong and Edwin Aldrin to the Apollo Command capsule for the return trip to earth.

[23] The Crazy World of Arthur Brown – "Fire" 1968
https://music.apple.com/us/album/fire/1577744761?i=1577744764

[24] Stevie Wonder – "My Cherie Amour" 1969
https://music.apple.com/us/album/my-cherie-amour/1442985614?i=1442985617

[25] The Classics IV – "Traces" 1969
https://music.apple.com/us/album/traces/724152155?i=724152398

[26] Young-Holt Unlimited – "Soulful Strut" 1969
https://music.apple.com/us/album/soulful-strut/115214079?i=115213775

[27] The Rolling Stones – "Jumpin' Jack Flash" 1968
https://music.apple.com/us/album/jumpin-jack-flash/1440764786?i=1440765744

[28] Hugo Montenegro – "The Good, the Bad, and the Ugly" 1969
https://music.apple.com/us/album/the-good-the-bad-and-the-ugly/254637060?i=254637065

[29] Before WWII broke out, to protect shipping from German U boats, the Navy placed a gun battery, consisting of two twelve-inch guns on the west beach of the Cape, not far from the Coast Guard station.

[30] The Ventures – "Pipeline" 1963
https://music.apple.com/us/album/pipeline/1444114461?i=1444114582

[31] Three Dog Night - "One" 1969
https://music.apple.com/us/album/one-single-version/1443771331?i=1443771335

[32] Herb Albert – "This Guy's in Love with You" 1968
https://music.apple.com/us/album/this-guys-in-love-with-you/1530056219?i=1530056874

[33] The Vogues – "You Are My Special Angel" 1966
https://music.apple.com/us/album/my-special-angel/289069214?i=289069477

[34] The Coca-Cola house was once the residence of an eastern North Carolina Coca-Cola bottler. The house originally served as a lifesaving station just east of the lighthouse. It was moved to its

201

current spot some seventy years earlier. The liberal use of Coca-Cola-red paint suggested it had been acquired at low cost.

[35] Steam – "Na Na Hey Hey, Kiss Him Goodbye" 1968
https://music.apple.com/us/album/na-na-hey-hey-kiss-him-goodbye/1434901719?i=1434901987

[36] Steppenwolf – "Magic Carpet Ride" 1968
https://music.apple.com/us/album/magic-carpet-ride/1425254822?i=1425255189

[37] "Spotting a train one day on a bombing run, I asked for and got permission to destroy it. I circled around behind the train while diving down to 200 yards – that's where the rounds of six .50 caliber wing guns converge. Closing in on the end of the train, I began firing my guns sending wood, metal, and covers flying into the air. When I hit the fuel and munition cars, fire and hot gas darkened by canopy with soot, but not so much that I couldn't finish my run to destroy the locomotive."

[38] Our planes had an 8 MM camera that started filming when pilots hit the gun trigger.

[39] "I had engine failure one time over Yugoslavia's Mediterranean coast, in the middle of winter. I found myself having to choose between a rocky landing that would surely mean a crackup or ditching in the icy waters of the Mediterranean in which hypothermia would get me in minutes. I saw people on the coast but didn't see how they could get to me fast enough."

Just before I lost too much altitude to make it, I spotted a road on the side of the cliff with enough of a straightaway for a landing. Approaching the downwind side of the road in a steep turn and bank to drop as much speed as possible, I leveled the wings when I was lined up with the road. I immediately lost both wings and landing gear as they struck the mountainside on the right and the guardrail on the left. I continued skidding down the road in my fuselage until I ran head-on into a ten-wheel truck. My long engine in front protected me, but the driver, a British serviceman, wasn't so lucky."

[40] Dione Warwick – "I'll Never Fall in Love Again" 1969
https://music.apple.com/us/album/ill-never-fall-in-love-again/40284673?i=40284677

[41] The Fifth Dimension – "The Age of Aquarius" 1969
https://music.apple.com/us/album/aquarius-let-the-sunshine-in/303078879?i=303078892

[42] The Ventures – "Pipeline" 1963
https://music.apple.com/us/album/pipeline/1444114461?i=1444114582

[43] A-Frame waves have perfectly defined peaks that peal and break equally left and right. Both directions offer equally good opportunities for surfers.

[44] The Surfaris – "Wipeout" 1963
https://music.apple.com/us/album/wipe-out-hit-version/1354226132?i=1354226233

[45] The Rivieras – "California Sun" 1964
https://music.apple.com/us/album/california-sun/1146567915?i=1146567916

[46] The Endless Summer Directed by Bruce Brown, Producers Bruce Brown and Robert Bagley, Bruce Brown Films, 1966

[47] The Rolling Stones – "Jumping Jack Flash" 1969
https://music.apple.com/us/album/california-sun/1146567915?i=1146567916

[48] Jay and the Americans – "Hushabye" 1969
https://music.apple.com/us/album/hushabye/715466840?i=715467102

[49] Donovan – "Atlantis" 1968
https://music.apple.com/us/album/atlantis/186225163?i=186225443

Disclosure One: The character Tracy, the events involving her, and the place of her introduction are all fictional to protect a real person from unnecessary attention or embarrassment. The character Tracy and her interactions with young Sam are emblematic of a true person and my subsequent yearnings for her and love itself. Both seemed equally, beyond my reach.

Disclosure Two: The Tropical Storm Eve was an actual weather event at the end of the summer, but it is used in the story as a device to huddle the boys physically and emotionally through a crisis. The heightened tension provides perfect conditions in which the boys found it easy to share their deepest hurts—the pain of which had become apparent to the others during the summer. The issues covered were real and pervasive, but for the sake of story, a climactic finish was more poignant and fitting. Surfing was more prevalent in the story than in our activities as presented. Good surfing was the reason to stay on the island longer for the tropical storm.